faith first

Legacy Edition

PARISH

Grade Three

RESOURCES FOR CHRISTIAN LIVING®

www.FaithFirst.com

"The Ad Hoc Committee to Oversee the Use of the Catechism, United States Conference of Catholic Bishops, has found this catechetical series, copyright 2006, to be in conformity with the *Catechism of the Catholic Church*."

NIHIL OBSTAT
Reverend Robert M. Coerver
Censor Librorum

IMPRIMATUR
† Most Rev. Charles V. Grahmann
Bishop of Dallas

September 1, 2004

The Nihil Obstat and Imprimatur are official declarations that the material reviewed is free of doctrinal or moral error. No implication is contained therein that those granting the Nihil Obstat and Imprimatur agree with the contents, opinions, or statements expressed.

Send all inquiries to:
RCL • Resources for Christian Living
200 East Bethany Drive
Allen, Texas 75002-3804

Toll Free   877-275-4725
Fax   800-688-8356

Visit us at www.RCLweb.com
              www.FaithFirst.com

Printed in the United States of America

20473   ISBN 0-7829-1065-3 (Student Book)

20483   ISBN 0-7829-1077-7 (Catechist Guide)

2 3 4 5 6 7 8 9 10 11
06 07 08 09 10 11 12

ACKNOWLEDGMENTS

Scripture excerpts are taken or adapted from the *New American Bible with Revised New Testament and Psalms* Copyright © 1991, 1986, 1970, Confraternity of Christian Doctrine, Washington, DC. Used with permission. All rights reserved. No part of the *New American Bible* may be reproduced by any means without the permission of the copyright owner.

Excerpts are taken or adapted from the English translation of the *Roman Missal* © 1973, International Committee on English in the Liturgy, Inc. (ICEL); the English translation of the Act of Contrition from *Rite of Penance* © 1974, ICEL; the English translation of *Rite of Confirmation, Second Edition* © 1975, ICEL; excerpts from the English translation of *A Book of Prayers* © 1982, ICEL; excerpts from the English translation of *Book of Blessings* © 1988, ICEL. All rights reserved.

Excerpts are taken or adapted from the English translation of *Gloria Patri*, The Nicene Creed, The Apostles' Creed, *Sanctus*, and *Agnus Dei*, by the International Consultation on English Texts (ICET).

Photograph and Illustration Credits appear on page 304.

Faith First Legacy Edition Development Team

Developing a religion program requires the gifts and talents of many individuals working together as a team. RCL is proud to acknowledge the contributions of these dedicated people.

Program Theology Consultants
Reverend Louis J. Cameli, S.T.D.
Reverend Robert D. Duggan, S.T.D.

Advisory Board
Judith Deckers, M.Ed.
Elaine McCarron, SCN, M.Div.
Marina Herrera, Ph.D.
Reverend Frank McNulty, S.T.D.
Reverend Ronald J. Nuzzi, Ph.D.

National Catechetical Advisor
Jacquie Jambor

Catechetical Specialist
Jo Rotunno

Contributing Writers
Student Book and Catechist Guide
Christina DeCamp
Judith Deckers
Mary Beth Jambor
Marianne K. Lenihan
Michele Norfleet

Art & Design Director
Lisa Brent

Electronic Page Makeup
Laura Fremder

Production Director
Jenna Nelson

Designers/Photo Research
Pat Bracken
Kristy O. Howard
Susan Smith

Project Editors
Patricia A. Classick
Steven M. Ellair
Ronald C. Lamping

Web Site Producers
Joseph Crisalli
Demere Henson

General Editor
Ed DeStefano

President/Publisher
Maryann Nead

Contents

We Celebrate: The Liturgical Seasons

We Pray

Welcome to Faith First!

My Friends, My Family, and Me

Write your answers. Then tell your answers to someone you do not know very well.

My name is _JaRe_.

My friends call me _JaRe_.

I live with _LeJ Si DaJ moM sVll ross_.

My family and I have the most fun when we _go on vicationS_.

A game I like to play with my friends is _Footbal_.

My favorite story is _gooseBumps_.

The thing I like best about my church is _everytning_.

Learning About
the Catholic Church

The Church is like a house of faith. In each of the rooms we can learn more about what Catholics believe, how we celebrate, how Jesus calls us to live, and how we pray. Do the activity on these pages to discover some things we will learn about this year.

We Believe

Saint Paul the Apostle was an early Christian. He was a missionary who traveled to many places to spread the Good News.

Look on page 81. Find the name of an American missionary who made a difference. Write his name on the bottom step.

St. Jhon

We Worship

One way to worship God is to continue Jesus' work on earth. Two of the Church's sacraments help Christians serve the whole Church.

Look on pages 147 and 148. Write the names of the two sacraments on the lines below.

_____

_____

We Live

Our whole parish family helps to continue Jesus' work on earth through acts of service.

Look on page 177. Write two things that parishes do on the To Do list. Put a check next to one that you or your family could do.

To Do

❑ _____

_____

❑ _____

_____

We Pray

Catholics pray alone, with one another, with their families, and at Mass. The Hail Mary is a special Catholic prayer.

Look on page 227. Find out what Bible story the Hail Mary helps us remember. Write the name of the story and the two characters here.

Title: _____

Characters: _____

_____

A Community of Believers

LEADER: Lord, we gather to listen to your word. Help us remember how to live as members of your Church.

ALL: **Your word is truth and life.**

LEADER: A reading from the Acts of the Apostles.

The community of believers was of one heart and mind. They followed the Apostles and respected them. Everyone shared everything they had with those in need. One of the early Christians, Barnabas, sold his land and gave the money to the Apostles to help Christians in need.

Based on Acts of the Apostles 2:42, 45–47

The word of the Lord.

ALL: **Thanks be to God.**
Come forward and reverence the Bible by bowing before it.

Unit 1 • We Believe

What does the Church ask us to believe?

Getting Ready

What I Have Learned

What is something you already know about these three faith words?

The Holy Trinity

_____

_____

Jesus' death and Resurrection

_____

_____

The Church

_____

_____

Words to Know

Put an X next to the faith words you know. Put a ? next to the faith words you need to know more about.

Faith Words

_____X___ faith

_____ Holy Trinity

_____ divine Providence

_____ Incarnation

_____ Messiah

_____ Paschal Mystery

_____ Pentecost

_____ Church

Questions I Have

What questions would you like to ask about the Church?

_____

_____

A Scripture Story

The coming of the Holy Spirit

How did the Holy Spirit help the disciples?

God Speaks to Us

We Pray

LORD, my God,
 you are great!
Psalm 104:1

**Glory be
to the Father,
and to the Son,
and to the Holy
Spirit.   Amen.**

*How do you make
new friends and get
to know old friends
better?*

Friends spend time
talking together. They
share things and get
to know each other
better. God is always
inviting us to get to
know him better too.

*What are some of the
ways you can try to
know God better
this year?*

God Tells Us Who He Is

Faith Focus

What are some ways that God speaks to us?

Faith Words

faith
Faith is a gift from God. It helps us believe in God and all that he has revealed.

Holy Trinity
The Holy Trinity is the mystery of one God in three divine Persons—God the Father, God the Son, and God the Holy Spirit.

What prayer of the Church shows that there is one God in three Persons? Quietly pray that prayer in your heart.

Baptism of Jesus (Matthew 3:13–17)

God Tells Us About Himself

God is a mystery. A mystery is what we could never know on our own. God has to reveal, or tell us, about himself. God gives us the gift of **faith.** Faith helps us come to know and believe in God and what he reveals.

God has revealed that he is one God in three Persons. He is the **Holy Trinity.** The three divine Persons are God the Father, God the Son, and God the Holy Spirit. This is a great mystery of faith.

God Speaks to Us in the Bible

The Bible is the written word of God. The Holy Spirit helped God's people write the Bible. The Bible is also called Sacred Scripture. The words *Sacred Scripture* mean "holy writings." In the Bible we read,

Always remember that the holy writings come to us from God.

Based on 2 Timothy 3:15–16

The Old Testament is the first main part of the Bible. It tells us about the promises God made at creation and to Noah, Abraham, Moses, and the prophets. God always keeps his promises.

The New Testament is the second main part of the Bible. It tells us about Jesus and his teachings. Jesus tells us the most about God.

Write about your favorite Bible story that helps you learn about God. Share that story with a friend.

Faith-Filled People

The Evangelists

The writers of the four Gospels are called the four Evangelists. They are Saint Matthew, Saint Mark, Saint Luke, and Saint John.

God Speaks to Us through the Church

During his life on earth, Jesus called people to follow him. These followers of Jesus were called disciples. They were the first members of the Church. Jesus chose some of these followers to be the leaders of the Church. These were the Apostles.

The New Testament tells us,

Many people came to believe in Jesus. They listened to the teachings of the Apostles. They cared for one another. They prayed together. They broke bread together. Together they praised God.

Based on Acts of the Apostles 2:42, 45–47

We belong to the Catholic Church. The Catholic Church goes back to Jesus and the Apostles.

List three people in the Church who help you come to know God. Tell how they help you.

Names	How They Help
_____	_____
_____	_____
_____	_____

Christian Art

Christians have always shared their faith in God. One way they have shared their faith in God is through beautiful works of art. God can speak to us through religious art.

Christian artists create mosaics and stained-glass windows. They decorate churches and cathedrals. These and other works of Christian art express faith in Jesus. These works of art help people come to know, love, and serve God better.

Tell what each of the pictures shows about the faith of Christians in Jesus.

Our Catholic Faith

Statues

Statues are symbols of the faith of Christians. They help us remember Jesus and Mary and the saints. Statues of the saints give honor to them. We honor the saints because of their faith and holy lives.

Mosaic

Stained glass

Wood carving

17

What Difference Does Faith Make in My Life?

Many people help you come to know, love, and serve God. Most importantly, the Holy Spirit helps you.

Write about or draw yourself helping your family come to know God better.

Helping My Family

My Faith Choice

This week I will help my family to know God better. I will

_____

_____.

Praying the Creed

The Church prays the creed, or professes its faith, each Sunday at Mass. Pray these words from the Nicene Creed.

All: **We believe in one God, the Holy Trinity.**

Group 1: We believe in one God,
the Father, the Almighty,
maker of heaven and earth.

Group 2: We believe in one Lord, Jesus Christ,
the only Son of God.

Group 3: We believe in the Holy Spirit,
the Lord, the giver of life.

All: **We believe in one God, the Holy Trinity.**

We Remember

In each leaf of the shamrock, write one way you come to know God.

To Help You Remember

1. God gives us the gift of faith to help us know and believe in God.

2. God speaks to us through the Bible.

3. God speaks to us through the Church.

This Week . . .

In chapter 1, "God Speaks to Us," your child learned that God has revealed himself to us. God is a mystery, and we could not know many things about God unless God revealed them. Jesus revealed that there is one God in three Persons— God the Father, Son, and Holy Spirit. We call this mystery of God the Holy Trinity. This is the central belief of Christians. The Bible and the Church teach and help us understand what God has revealed.

For more on the teachings of the Catholic Church on divine Revelation and the mystery of the Holy Trinity, see *Catechism of the Catholic Church* paragraph numbers 232–260.

Sharing God's Word

Read together the Bible story in Acts 2:42–47 about the first members of the Church or read the adaptation of the story on page 16. Emphasize that the first Christians cared about one another and prayed together.

Praying

In this chapter your child learned part of the Nicene Creed. Read and pray together this part of the creed on page 19.

Making a Difference

Choose one of the following activities to do as a family or design a similar activity of your own.

- When you take part in Mass this week, plan to arrive early or stay late. Walk around the church and look at all the works of art in your parish. Talk together about what each work of art teaches you about God.

- Take time this week to become more familiar with the Apostles' Creed. You can find the creed on page 284. Use the Apostles' Creed for family prayer.

- Talk about how your family helps one another know God. Ask each family member to choose one thing they can do this week to help the rest of the family know God better.

For more ideas on ways your family can live your faith, visit the "Faith First for Families" page at **www.FaithFirst.com**. You will find the "About Your Child" page helpful as your child begins a new year.

God the Creator of Heaven and Earth

We Pray

LORD! . . .
the earth is full
of your creatures.
Psalm 104:24

**Blessed are you,
God, Creator of
heaven and earth.
Amen.**

*What parts of
creation do you enjoy
the most?*

God is the loving
Creator. God's
beautiful creation
tells us about his
goodness.

*What beautiful parts
of creation remind
you that God is good?*

God the Creator

Faith Focus

Why did God create the world and people?

Faith Words

creation
Creation is all that God has made out of love and without any help.

divine Providence
Divine Providence is God's caring love for all his creation.

In this space draw another gift of God's creation. Tell how it helps you come to know how wonderful and good God is.

A Loving Creator

We believe that God alone is the Creator. He created everything and everyone out of love and without any help. The Book of Genesis, the first book in the Old Testament, tells the story of **creation.** We read,

God made light. God made the earth and sky and sea. God filled the earth with plants. God made the sun and the moon and the stars. God made birds for the sky and fish for the water. God made animals for the land. Then God created people. God saw that his creation was very good.

Based on Genesis 1:3–27, 31

Through our eyes and other senses we can come to know that God is wonderful and good. All God's creation helps us know his love for us.

God Created People

God created every person. God created everyone to be different from one another in many ways. All our differences make us special.

God created every person to be the same in one very important way. God created each of us in his own image. Each of us is a child of God.

God made people in his image. He made them man and woman. God blessed them. God gave them the world to care for.

Based on Genesis 1:26–30

God created people with a body and a soul. Our soul is that part of us that lives forever. It gives us the power to know and love and serve God. By creating us in his own image, God gives us a wonderful responsibility. God calls us to love and care for his world.

Name two ways that you can care for God's world.

God Cares for His Creation

God our Father and Creator is with us at every moment. He provides for, or takes care of, his creation. We call God's caring love for his creation **divine Providence**.

Jesus revealed how much God cares for us. He said,

"Look at the fields of grass. God clothes the fields with beautiful wild flowers. Your Father in heaven knows everything you need."

Based on Matthew 6:30–32

God always cares for his creation. He cares for the least of his creation to the greatest of his creation. He cares about everything that happens in the world. We never have to handle our problems alone.

Decorate the border of the prayer with symbols of God's creation. Pray the prayer each morning.

God our Father and Creator, you care for me. I praise your name, O God. Amen.

Creation and Our Parish Church

God's beautiful creation fills our churches. The Church uses things from God's creation in our worship of God.

The bread and wine used at Mass come to us from the earth. Sometimes oil made from olives is used in our celebrations. Water is also often used. Water reminds us that God gives us new life in Jesus through Baptism.

The candles we use are often made from beeswax. In some churches, sunlight shines through stained-glass windows and fills our church with color. Our minds and hearts are lifted up to God in prayer.

All creation reminds us of God. We care for it as a special gift from God.

Look at these pictures of creation. Tell how they remind you of God's caring love.

Our Catholic Faith

Prayers of Blessing

The Church prays prayers of blessing. Prayers of blessing honor God as the source of all our blessings. They express our trust in God's loving care for us.

What Difference Does Faith Make in My Life?

God created you and all human beings and the universe out of love. The Holy Spirit shows you how to work with other people to care for creation. When you care for creation, you are thanking God for the gifts of creation.

Create a poster. Invite your friends to care for God's creation with you.

Caring for God's Creation

My Faith Choice

This week I will honor and bless God the Creator. I will take better care of God's gift of

_____

_____.

Praying a Psalm

Psalms are prayer songs. The Church prays the Psalms every day. Pray these verses from Psalm 104 together.

All: **Bless God. Our God, you are great!**

Group 1: You created all the creatures of the earth, in the oceans and in the sky.

Group 2: The earth is full of your creatures.

All: **Bless God. Our God, you are great!**

Based on Psalm 104:1, 24, 25

We Remember

Fill in the blanks. Use the words in the word bank to complete the faith sentences.

Blessing   soul   Providence   Creator

1. We believe that God is the
_____.

2. Divine _____ is God's caring love for all his creation.

3. God created people with a body and a
_____.

4. _____ prayers express our faith in God's loving care for us.

To Help You Remember

1. God created everyone and everything out of love and without any help.

2. God created every person in God's image and likeness.

3. God always cares for us and all of his creation.

This Week . . .

In chapter 2, "God the Creator of Heaven and Earth," your child came to know God as our loving, caring Creator. God's caring love is known as divine Providence. Everything and everyone God creates is good. God creates every person to be a unique individual. At the same time, God creates everyone in his own image and shares the very life of the Holy Trinity, sanctifying grace, with us.

For more on the teachings of the Catholic Church on the mysteries of God the Creator, see *Catechism of the Catholic Church* paragraph numbers 279–314, 325–349, and 355–379.

Sharing God's Word

Read together the Bible story in Genesis 1:1–31 about creation or read the adaptation of the story on page 22. Emphasize that the diversity within creation helps us come to know that God is wonderful and good.

Praying

In this chapter your child prayed part of Psalm 104. Read and pray together the adaptation of Psalm 104 on page 27. Or choose another psalm, look it up in the Bible, and pray it.

Making a Difference

Choose one of the following activities to do as a family or design a similar activity of your own.

- This week at Mass notice all of the things from creation your parish uses to help you worship. After Mass try to name everything you saw.

- Invite each family member to share how creation helps them feel close to God.

- We honor God when we care for creation. As a family choose one thing you will do this week to take care of creation.

For more ideas on ways your family can live your faith, visit the "Faith First for Families" page at **www.FaithFirst.com**. The "Make a Difference" page goes especially well with this chapter.

Mary Trusted in God

We Pray

"[M]y spirit rejoices in God my savior."
Luke 1:47

Hail Mary, full of grace, the Lord is with you! Blessed are you among women.
Amen.

What do you do when someone tells you good news?

Sometimes we can't sit still when we hear good news. The angel Gabriel brought Mary very good news from God.

What good news did the angel bring to Mary?

Mary, the mother of Jesus, the Mother of God

The Faith of Mary

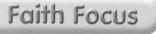

Faith Focus

How did Mary show her faith and trust in God?

Faith Words

Annunciation

The Annunciation is the announcement the angel Gabriel made to the Blessed Virgin Mary that God had chosen her to be the mother of Jesus, the Son of God.

Incarnation

The Incarnation is the Son of God becoming a man and still being God.

Retell the story of the Annunciation to a friend or a member of your family.

Mary and the angel Gabriel

Mary Says Yes to God

The best news that we will ever hear is that God sent his Son, Jesus, into our world. The angel Gabriel announced this good news to the Blessed Virgin Mary. Gabriel said,

"Hail, Mary. The Lord is with you. You shall give birth to a son and you shall name him Jesus. The Holy Spirit will come to you. Your son will be God's own Son." Based on Luke 1:28, 31, 35

The Church calls the announcement of Jesus' birth to Mary the **Annunciation.** Mary believed that God's word to her would come true. She had great faith in God's love for her.

Mary Praises God

Before Jesus was born, Mary visited a relative whose name was Elizabeth. Elizabeth was going to have a baby too. Mary's visit to Elizabeth is known as the Visitation.

When Mary arrived at Elizabeth's home, Elizabeth said, "Blessed are you, Mary!" Mary answered Elizabeth by praising God. Mary said, "My soul praises the great goodness of God! God has done great things for me!"

Based on Luke 1:46, 49

The Church calls Mary's prayer of praise of God the Magnificat. The Magnificat is a canticle, or song of praise to God.

Mary shows us what it means to believe and trust God with our whole heart. Mary is our model of faith.

Faith-Filled People

Elizabeth

Saint Elizabeth and Zechariah were the parents of John the Baptist. As Mary did, they trusted in God's promise to send God's people the Savior. Their son John grew up to announce the good news that Jesus was the Savior promised by God. The Church celebrates the feast day of Saint Elizabeth on November 5.

Write your own prayer of praise. Thank God for something wonderful he has done for you.

My Prayer of Praise

_____

_____

_____

_____

_____

Jesus Is Born

The Bible tells us that after Adam and Eve sinned, God promised to send a savior. God chose Mary to be the mother of the Savior he promised to send. The Holy Spirit helped Mary come to believe in God. Mary trusted in God's plans for her and her only son, Jesus.

When the time was right, Jesus, the Son of God and the son of Mary, was born according to God's plan. We call the Son of God becoming one of us and still being God the **Incarnation.**

We read the story of Jesus' birth in the Gospels of Matthew and Luke in the New Testament. The Church calls the story of the birth of Jesus the Nativity.

Pretend you are a news reporter on location in Bethlehem. You visit the manger. Report what you see and hear.

News Flash!

We interrupt this program to bring you this news bulletin.

_____

_____

_____

_____

_____

_____

_____

_____

Our Church Makes a Difference

We Honor Mary

Catholics honor Mary as the greatest saint. Mary is our model of faith. Mary's faith and trust in God help us know how to live as God's children.

Catholics show their devotion, or their love and respect, for Mary in many ways. Each year we celebrate feast days to honor Mary. On all these days we thank and praise God for choosing Mary to be the mother of his Son.

We also say special prayers to Mary. We place statues and pictures of Mary in our churches and homes. When we show our devotion to Mary, we show the world how much God loves all people.

What do these pictures tell you about Mary?

Our Catholic Faith

Feast Days of Mary

These are some of the feast days the Church celebrates to honor Mary.

January 1—Mary, Mother of God
May 31—Visitation
August 15—Assumption of Mary to Heaven
September 8—Birth of Mary
October 7—Our Lady of the Rosary
December 8—Immaculate Conception
December 12—Our Lady of Guadalupe

What Difference Does Faith Make in My Life?

Mary is the mother of the Church. She is our mother too. Mary wants you to believe in God and trust and love God with all your heart.

Design a poster with words and pictures that show ways you trust God and say yes to him.

Saying Yes to God

My Faith Choice

This week I will show my faith and trust in God. I will

_____

_____.

We Pray

The Angelus

The Angelus is a prayer that expresses the Church's faith that the Son of God became one of us and that Mary is the Mother of God.

Group1: The angel spoke God's message to Mary,

Group2: and she conceived of the Holy Spirit.

All: **Hail Mary . . .**

Group1: "I am the lowly servant of the Lord:

Group2: let it be done to me according to your word."

All: **Hail Mary . . .**

Group1: And the Word became flesh

Group2: and lived among us.

All: **Hail Mary . . .**

We Remember

Unscramble the blue letters to find the words that complete the sentences. Write the words on the lines.

1. The Son of God becoming man is called the **CANRAONINIT**.

_____

2. The announcement of the birth of Jesus to the Virgin Mary is called the **NNUANIOTIACN**.

_____

3. Mary's visit to Elizabeth is called the **ITOVSIATNI**.

_____

To Help You Remember

1. Mary believed that God had chosen her to be the mother of Jesus, the Son of God.

2. Mary praised God for choosing her to be the mother of the Savior.

3. Mary showed us what it means to believe and trust in God.

With My Family

This Week . . .

In chapter 3, "Mary Trusted in God," your child listened to the Bible stories of the Annunciation, the Visitation, and the Nativity. Mary believed and trusted in God. God chose Mary as part of his plan to fulfill his promise to send the world a savior. Mary is the mother of Jesus, the Son of God, the Savior of the world. He is the Savior whom God promised to send.

For more on the teachings of the Catholic Church on the mystery of the Incarnation and the unique role of Mary in God's plan for the salvation of the world, see *Catechism of the Catholic Church* paragraph numbers 456–478 and 484–507.

Sharing God's Word

Read the Bible story in Luke 1:26–38 about the angel Gabriel's announcement to Mary or read the adaptation of the story on page 30. Emphasize Mary's faith and trust in God and her love for him.

Praying

In this chapter your child learned to pray part of the Angelus. Read and pray together the Angelus on page 35.

Making a Difference

Choose one of the following activities to do as a family or design a similar activity of your own.

- Help each other become more familiar with the Hail Mary. Make puzzles of the prayer. Write the Hail Mary on a piece of paper. Cut the paper into small puzzle pieces. Then put the puzzle together. Assembling the puzzle will help you learn the prayer.

- Elizabeth and Zechariah were the parents of John the Baptist. Their son grew up to announce the good news that Jesus was the Savior promised by God. Read about Elizabeth and Zechariah in Luke 1:5–25.

- Mary believed in and trusted God. Talk about how your family shows that you believe in and trust God. Invite each person to share one thing they will do this week to show their belief and trust in God.

For more ideas on ways your family can live your faith, visit the "Faith First for Families" page at **www.FaithFirst.com**. Share some of the ideas on the "Gospel Reflections" page with one another this week.

Women of Faith
A Scripture Story

Queen Esther and the king of Persia

4

We Pray

Sing to the LORD,
  for he is glorious!
    Based on Exodus 15:1

Lord, we give our hearts to you. We trust you. We love you.   Amen.

Who do you know who has faith in God?

The Bible tells us about many men and women who had great faith in God.

What Bible stories have you heard about people of faith?

Bible Background

Faith Focus

How did women of the Old Testament show their faith in God?

Faith Words

trust

To trust someone is to know that what the person tells us is true and that the person will always do what is good for us.

Hannah

Sarah

Ruth

Sarah, Hannah, and Ruth

Mary, Jesus' mother, learned about God by hearing the stories of the Scriptures of the Jewish people. Mary heard the stories about Sarah, Hannah, and Ruth.

Sarah believed God's promise to her and gave birth to Isaac. Isaac became one of the great leaders of God's people. Hannah prayed to God for a child. Soon Hannah gave birth to Samuel. He became one of the judges of Israel. Ruth left her home to care for her husband's mother, Naomi, after both their husbands died.

Sarah, Hannah, and Ruth believed in God and had **trust** in his love. These women were models of faith for Mary and the Jewish people. They are models of faith for us too.

Find and circle the words in the puzzle that describe a person of faith.

X L M T F Q B
C O U R A G E
B V R U I L I
Q E T S T O E
G H D T H A F

Queen Esther

In Old Testament times God's people were sometimes forced to live away from their homeland. One time some Jewish people were forced to live in the ancient country of Persia.

Esther was a Jewish woman who became queen of that country. When she learned about a plot to kill her people, Queen Esther prayed,

"My LORD, you alone are God. Help me, for I am alone and I have no help but you. O God, remember us here. Save your people."

Based on Esther C:14, 25

With great courage, Esther told the king about the plot to kill her people. The king believed Esther, and God's people were saved. Each year the Jewish people remember and celebrate Queen Esther's faith and courage on the feast of Purim.

Think of someone or a group of people who is suffering. Quietly ask God to help them trust in his love for them.

Praying the Scriptures

Mary listened to the stories of her people. Listening to the stories of the faith-filled women helped Mary become a woman of faith. From these people of faith Mary learned what it means to believe and trust in God.

Christians today prayerfully listen to the stories of the Old Testament and the New Testament. We continue to follow the examples of many of the faith-filled women of the Bible. Listening to the stories of these women helps us grow in faith and trust in God.

Under each picture, write how the people are living as people of faith.

_____

_____

_____

_____

_____

_____

Blessed Teresa of Calcutta

Blessed Teresa of Calcutta was a religious sister and a woman of faith. For over fifty years she took care of people who were homeless, sick, and dying in the city of Calcutta in India.

Many women and men wanted to join Mother Teresa in her work. She started the Missionaries of Charity. Today more than 4,000 women and men religious and 10,000 volunteers continue her work of prayer and of service to the poor. In 1997 Mother Teresa died in Calcutta at the age of 87.

In 1979 she was given the Nobel Peace Prize because of her service to the poor and suffering in the world. In 2003 Pope John Paul II beatified Mother Teresa. The Church now honors her as Blessed Teresa.

Why do you think so many men and women have chosen to continue the hard work of Blessed Mother Teresa?

Our Catholic Faith

Prayer of the Faithful

At every Mass we celebrate the Liturgy of the Word. We listen to the Scriptures, profess our faith in God, and pray the Prayer of the Faithful. As God's people, we open our hearts to God in faith and trust as Mary, Queen Esther, and Blessed Teresa of Calcutta did.

Blessed Mother Teresa talking with two blind children

41

What Difference Does Faith Make in My Life?

God gives you the gift of faith. The Holy Spirit and people of faith help you grow in faith. You show your faith by the way you act and pray.

Draw or write about a person of faith who has helped you grow in faith.

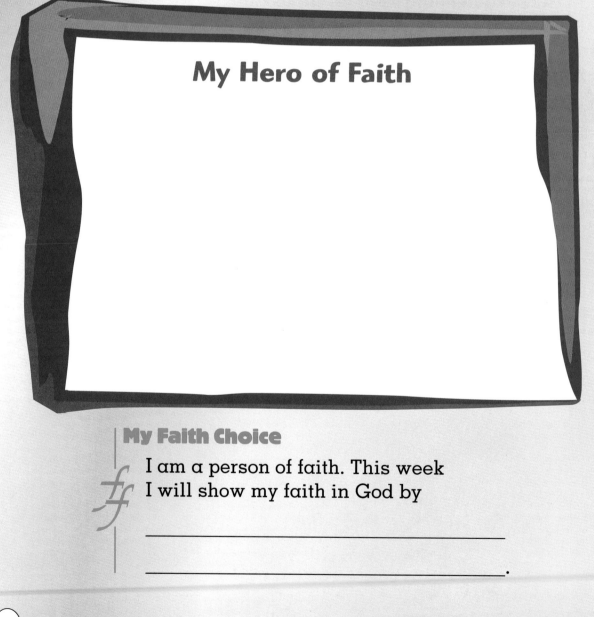

My Hero of Faith

My Faith Choice

I am a person of faith. This week I will show my faith in God by

_____

_____.

We Pray

Litany of the Saints

Catholics pray to the saints. Pray part of the Litany of the Saints together.

Leader: Holy Mary, Mother of God   **All:** pray for us.

Leader: Our Lady of Guadalupe   **All:** pray for us.

Leader: All you holy women
of the Old Testament   **All:** pray for us.

Leader: Saint Elizabeth Ann Seton   **All:** pray for us.

Leader: Saint Katharine Drexel   **All:** pray for us.

Leader: Blessed Teresa of Calcutta   **All:** pray for us.

All: *Add your own saint.*   **All:** pray for us.

We Remember

Choose one of the women of faith you learned about in this chapter. In this space describe why she is honored as a woman of faith.

To Help You Remember

1. Sarah and Hannah lived lives of faith and trust in God.

2. Ruth put her faith and trust in God and helped Naomi.

3. Queen Esther prayed and asked God to save her people.

This Week . . .

In chapter 4, "Women of Faith: A Scripture Story," your child listened to Bible stories from the Old Testament about women of faith: Sarah, Hannah, Ruth, and Queen Esther. These women of faith trusted God's love and prayed for God's help. Prayers of intercession were common to all these women. They prayed with deep trust in God. Hearing the stories of the faith-filled women of the Old Testament helped Mary become a woman of faith. The lives of the women and the lives of all the saints help us live a faith-filled life.

For more on the teachings of the Catholic Church on Sacred Scripture and the saints, see *Catechism of the Catholic Church* paragraph numbers 101–133 and 144–175.

Sharing God's Word

Read together the Bible story in Esther C:14–25 or the adaptation of the story on page 39. Emphasize that Queen Esther's faith and trust in God helped her people in their time of suffering.

Praying

In this chapter your child learned to pray part of the Litany of the Saints. Read and pray together the prayer on page 43.

Making a Difference

Choose one of the following activities to do as a family or design a similar activity of your own.

- Hannah, Sarah, Ruth, and Esther were models of faith for Mary. Invite each family member to share three people who have been models of faith for them. Be sure they explain why they chose each person.

- Make a faith tree. On the leaves of your faith tree, write the names of all of the people who have helped your family believe and trust in God.

- Choose one of the names from the Litany of the Saints on page 43. Find out more about this saint. You can look on the Internet, at the public library, or in your parish library.

For more ideas on ways your family can live your faith, visit the "Faith First for Families" page at **www.FaithFirst.com**. Click on the "Saints" page and discover other faith-filled people of the Church.

Jesus, the Son of God

We Pray

Help us, God our
   savior,
   for the glory of your
   name.   Psalm 79:9

**God of love
and mercy,
open our hearts
to welcome
Jesus with joy.
            Amen.**

*Has anyone ever
saved you from
danger?*

*God promised to
send a savior to save
us from our sins.*

*Who did God send to
be the Savior?*

*Christ and the Children of All
Races by V. Horio Bianchini* (45)

The Good News of Jesus Christ

Faith Focus

What is the Good News of Jesus Christ?

Faith Words

Jesus
The name *Jesus* means "God saves." Jesus is the Son of God and the Savior that God promised to send his people.

Messiah
The word *messiah* means "anointed one." Jesus is the Messiah, the Anointed One of God, the Savior God promised to send.

Jesus Is the Messiah

The angel Gabriel told Mary to name her baby **Jesus.** The name *Jesus* means "God saves." Jesus is the Savior God promised to send his people.

Soon after Jesus was born, Mary and Joseph took Jesus to the Temple in Jerusalem to dedicate him to God. Christians call this event in the life of Jesus the Presentation of the Lord.

When the Holy Family arrived at the Temple, they met Simeon and Anna. Simeon and Anna had been waiting all their lives for the **Messiah,** the Savior God promised to send. Simeon took Jesus in his arms, blessed God, and said,

"O God, my eyes have now seen your salvation." Based on Luke 2:30

Pretend you are in the Temple. How would you greet the Holy Family?

The Holy Family

When Jesus was twelve years old, the Holy Family went to Jerusalem to celebrate Passover. Passover is a feast that the Jewish people celebrate each year. It celebrates God's mercy and love for his people. It especially celebrates God's freeing his people from slavery in Egypt.

When the Passover feast was over, Mary and Joseph could not find Jesus. The Bible tells us what happened.

After searching the city for three days, Mary and Joseph found Jesus in the Temple. He was sitting with the teachers, listening to them and asking them questions.

Jesus returned home to Nazareth with Mary and Joseph. He remained obedient to them. As the years passed, Jesus grew in wisdom, age, and grace.

Based on Luke 2:46–47, 51–52

Follow the maze. Help Mary and Joseph find Jesus and bring him back home to Nazareth.

The First Shall Be Last, painting by French artist James Tissot (1836–1902)

Jesus Brings Good News

Jesus left his home in Nazareth when he was about thirty years old. Traveling from place to place, Jesus spent much of his time teaching people the good news of the kingdom of God.

Many people listened to Jesus and became his disciples. A disciple is a person who learns from and follows the teachings of another person. That is why Jesus' disciples called him Rabbi, or Teacher.

Jesus' disciples came to believe that Jesus Christ was the Son of God and the Messiah. The name *Christ* means "Anointed One" and "Messiah."

Write two words that describe a good disciple.

A Good Disciple

Good News in Action

The third grade class at Saint Monica's Parish wanted to continue the work that Jesus began. They wanted to prepare the way for the coming of the kingdom of God. They thought about collecting food and clothing for the poor. They considered sending get-well cards to people who were sick. Finally, they decided to collect food when they heard the town food pantry was almost empty.

The class made posters to get other people involved. On the day of the collection, more than fifty people came to help. They filled twenty-eight boxes with food.

Describe one way that you can work with your friends to continue the work Jesus began.

Our Catholic Faith

Holy Childhood Association

The Holy Childhood Association helps young Catholics spread the Good News of Jesus. Children in religious education programs and in Catholic schools collect money. The money is used to provide food, clean water, medicine, places to live, and education to poor children in more than one hundred countries.

What Difference Does Faith Make in My Life?

Each time you put your faith in Jesus into action you announce the Good News announced by Jesus. You live the Gospel. You prepare for the coming of the kingdom of God.

Complete the survey. Circle the things that disciples of Jesus can do to live the Gospel today. Then discuss with a group some times and places you could do one of these things.

Disciples of Jesus Today

1. Come to know Jesus by reading the Bible.

Agree   **Disagree**

2. Welcome children who are new to our school or neighborhood.

Agree   **Disagree**

3. Help out at home more often.

Agree   **Disagree**

My Faith Choice

This week I will try to live as a disciple of Jesus. I will live the Gospel by

_____

_____.

We Pray

Lord, Have Mercy

At Mass we ask God to bless us with the gift of his mercy. Pray this prayer, which we sometimes pray in the Introductory Rites of the Mass.

Leader: Lord Jesus, you came to gather all people into the peace of God's kingdom.

All: **Lord, have mercy.**

Leader: You come in word and sacrament to strengthen us in holiness.

All: **Christ, have mercy.**

Leader: You will come in glory with salvation for all your people.

All: **Lord, have mercy.**

We Remember

Match the people and places in the left column with the meanings in the right column.

People and Places

_____ **1.** Anna and Simeon

_____ **2.** disciples

_____ **3.** kingdom of God

_____ **4.** Jerusalem

Meanings

a. People who are followers of Jesus

b. The holy city of the Jewish people

c. The good news of God's mercy and love

d. People who recognized the infant Jesus to be the Messiah

To Help You Remember

1. Jesus Christ is the Messiah, the Savior God promised to send.

2. Jesus obeyed Mary and Joseph and grew in wisdom, age, and grace.

3. Jesus announced the good news of the kingdom of God.

With My Family

This Week . . .

In chapter 5, "Jesus, the Son of God," your child learned that God sent Jesus Christ as the Messiah. He is the One anointed by the Holy Spirit to announce and share God's mercy and love with God's people. He is the Savior of the world. When Jesus was a baby, Mary and Joseph took him to the Temple in Jerusalem and dedicated him to God. At the Temple, Simeon and Anna recognized Jesus to be the Messiah. Life in the Holy Family prepared Jesus for his work as the Messiah. When he grew up, Jesus left his home in Nazareth, called disciples to follow him, and traveled about announcing the coming of the kingdom of God.

For more on the teachings of the Catholic Church on the mysteries of the infancy, hidden life, and public life of Christ, see *Catechism of the Catholic Church* paragraph numbers 512–560.

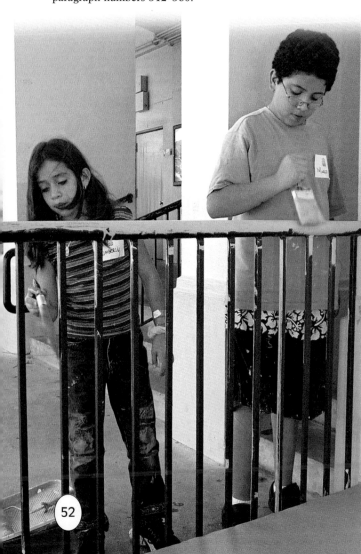

Sharing God's Word

Read together the Bible story in Luke 2:42–47, 51–52 about Jesus in the Temple or read the adaptation of the story on page 47. Emphasize that as Jesus grew up, he grew in wisdom and in faith.

Praying

In this chapter your child learned responses from the Act of Penitence we sometimes pray during the Introductory Rites of the Mass. In this prayer we ask God to bless us with his gift of mercy. Read and pray the prayer on page 51.

Making a Difference

Choose one of the following activities to do as a family or design a similar activity of your own.

- Talk about what it means to live as a disciple of Jesus. As a family, choose one thing you can do together this week to live as disciples of Jesus.

- When you take part in Mass this week, pay close attention to the response "Lord, have mercy" at the beginning of Mass. Use the response as your family prayer this week. Remember that God's mercy is a gift.

- Read together the Beatitudes on page 286. Talk about how living the Beatitudes prepares for the coming of the kingdom of God that Jesus announced.

For more ideas on ways your family can live your faith, visit the "Faith First for Families" page at **www.FaithFirst.com**. Visit the "Games" page. Ask your child to show you the game they most like.

Jesus' Death and Resurrection

We Pray

LORD, bless us with
your kindness.
We hope in you.

Based on Psalm 33:22

**God our Father,
you raised Jesus
from the dead.
Give us the gift
of eternal life.**

Amen.

*How does it feel when
someone forgives you?*

Forgiveness is a sign
of love. Jesus died on
the cross to forgive
our sins and make us
sharers in God's
forgiving love.

*What do you know
about the death and
Resurrection of Jesus?*

Jesus Dies and Is Risen

Faith Focus

What does the Paschal Mystery of Jesus tell us about God's love?

Faith Words

Paschal Mystery
The Paschal Mystery is the Passion, death, Resurrection, and Ascension of Jesus Christ.

Jesus Dies on the Cross

After Jesus ate the Last Supper with his disciples, Judas brought the soldiers to arrest Jesus. The soldiers then brought Jesus to Pontius Pilate. Pilate ordered Jesus to be crucified, or put to death on a cross. This is what happened next.

The soldiers led Jesus outside of Jerusalem and nailed him onto a cross. Before he died, Jesus said, "Father, forgive them." At about three o'clock in the afternoon, Jesus said in a loud voice, "Father, I now give myself to you." Based on Luke 23:26, 33–34, 44, 46

The death of Jesus on the cross is called the Crucifixion.

Jesus sacrificed his life to save all people from their sins so that we could live forever in heaven. The word *sacrifice* means "to give something that we value to God out of love."

Why do we call Jesus' dying on a cross "the sacrifice of the cross"?

Mary watching as Jesus passes by carrying his cross

God Raises Jesus to New Life

When Jesus died on the cross, Jesus' disciples thought they lost someone they loved. Three days later, they received some amazing good news. Here is their story.

After Jesus died on the cross, his disciple Joseph of Arimathea laid his body in his tomb. Three days later some of the women disciples of Jesus went to the tomb where he was buried. When the women looked in the tomb, Jesus' body was not there. The angel announced, "God has raised Jesus from the dead! Tell the other disciples to go to Galilee. Jesus will meet them there."

Based on Matthew 27:59–60; 28:1, 5–7

This event is called the Resurrection.

Jesus' suffering, death, Resurrection, and Ascension are known as the **Paschal Mystery.** It is the passover of Jesus from death to new life. Jesus won for us the promise of life everlasting with God. We believe that we too shall live after we die. We will live in happiness with God forever.

Create a two-sentence verse announcing the Resurrection.

Joyful People!

_____

_____

_____

_____

_____

_____

55

Jesus Returns to His Father

After he was raised from the dead, Jesus came to the disciples and stayed with them for forty days. When the time came for Jesus to return to his Father in heaven, this is what happened.

Jesus blessed his disciples and sent them to share the Good News with the whole world. The Risen Jesus was then taken into heaven.

Based on Luke 24:50–51

We call Jesus' return to his Father the Ascension. The word *ascension* means "a going up." One day we too will return to our Father in heaven.

Design this emblem with symbols or words that tell about the Paschal Mystery of Jesus Christ.

The Way of the Cross

You see the Way of the Cross, or the Stations of the Cross, in Catholic Churches. Catholics pray the Stations of the Cross as a community during the season of Lent. Praying the Way of the Cross helps us remember Jesus' suffering, death, and Resurrection. It helps us live Jesus' command, "Love one another as I have loved you" (based on John 13:34).

Turn to page 289 and prayerfully read the list of the Stations of the Cross. Thank Jesus for his love for you and for all people.

Our Catholic Faith

The Easter Candle

The lighted Easter candle reminds us that Jesus was raised from the dead. We see the Easter candle in the place where the Church baptizes people and near the altar.

First Station: Jesus condemned to death

Fifth Station: Simon helping Jesus carry the cross

Twelfth Station: Death of Jesus on the cross

What Difference Does Faith Make in My Life?

At Baptism you were made a sharer in Jesus' Paschal Mystery. You received the gift of the Holy Spirit. The Holy Spirit gives you the courage to make sacrifices to help other people. The Holy Spirit helps you love others as Jesus commanded.

Complete each sentence. Write what a true disciple of Jesus would do.

New Life!

When I see someone who is sad, I will_____

_____.

When I see someone who is _____, I will _____

_____.

When I see someone who is _____, I will _____

_____.

My Faith Choice

This week I will show that I share in the Paschal Mystery of Jesus. I will

_____

_____.

Praying the Scriptures

We can use our imagination when we read and pray the Scriptures. We call this a prayer of meditation.

Leader: Close your eyes as I read a Gospel story about the Resurrection. Picture yourself in the room with the disciples.
A reading from the holy gospel according to Matthew. *Read Matthew 28:1–10.*

All: **Glory to you, O Lord.**

Leader: The Gospel of the Lord.

All: **Praise to you, Lord Jesus Christ.**

Leader: Talk with Jesus. *(Pause.)* Open your eyes. Let us all thank God.

We Remember

Unscramble the blue letters to find the words that complete the sentences. Write the words on the lines.

1. Jesus' death on the cross is the **ciCruionfix.**

   _____

2. Jesus' being raised by God to new life is the **surrecRetion.**

   _____

3. Jesus' return to his Father in heaven is the **sionAscen.**

   _____

To Help You Remember

1. Jesus suffered and died on the cross to save all people from their sins.

2. Three days after Jesus died and was buried, God raised Jesus from the dead.

3. Forty days after he was raised from the dead, the Risen Jesus ascended, or returned, to his Father in heaven.

This Week . . .

In chapter 6, "Jesus' Death and Resurrection," your child learned about the Paschal Mystery of Jesus. The Paschal Mystery is the Passion, death, Resurrection, and Ascension of Jesus Christ. At Baptism we are made sharers in the Paschal Mystery of Jesus. We receive the promise of eternal life in heaven. Jesus suffered and died on the cross and was raised from the dead to save all people from sin. Forty days after the Resurrection Jesus returned, or ascended, to his Father. We await Christ's return in glory at the end of time when the kingdom he proclaimed will fully come about. We show our belief in these events by the way we live Jesus' new commandment of love.

For more on the teachings of the Catholic Church on the mystery of Christ's Passion, death, Resurrection, and Ascension, see *Catechism of the Catholic Church* paragraph numbers 599–655.

Sharing God's Word

Read together the Bible story in Luke 23:24–46 about Jesus' Crucifixion and burial or read the adaptation of the story on page 54. Emphasize that even as Jesus was dying, he forgave those who had put him to death.

Praying

In this chapter your child prayed the Scriptures. Read and pray together the prayer on page 59.

Making a Difference

Choose one of the following activities to do as a family or design a similar activity of your own.

- Read together the Bible story about Jesus' Resurrection on page 55. Talk about how the women must have felt when they found the empty tomb.

- The Easter candle reminds us that the Risen Christ is with us. When you take part in Mass, look for the Easter candle.

- The next time you go to church, take some time to visit your parish's Stations of the Cross. Talk about what each station tells about Jesus' great love for your family and for all people.

For more ideas on ways your family can live your faith, visit the "Faith First for Families" page at **www.FaithFirst.com**. You will find the "Contemporary Issues" page helpful this week.

The Holy Spirit
A Scripture Story

We Pray

Thus says the LORD God: . . . I will put my spirit within you.

Ezekiel 36:23, 27

Come, Holy Spirit, fill our hearts with the fire of your love. Amen.

When have you felt better when someone was with you to help and guide you?

Jesus promised that the Holy Spirit would always be with the Church after he returned to his Father in heaven.

What do you know about the Holy Spirit?

Dove and flames of fire, symbols of the Holy Spirit

61

Bible Background

Faith Words

Holy Spirit

The Holy Spirit is the third Person of the Holy Trinity.

Pentecost

Pentecost is the day on which the Holy Spirit came to the disciples of Jesus in Jerusalem fifty days after the Resurrection.

Jesus Promises the Holy Spirit

At the Last Supper Jesus told his disciples that he was going to return to his Father. Then he told them not to worry or be sad. Jesus promised that he would not leave them alone.

Jesus promised that God would send the **Holy Spirit** to his disciples. The Holy Spirit is the third Person of the Holy Trinity. The Holy Spirit would help them remember all that Jesus taught them. The Holy Spirit would always be with them. They would never be alone.

After Jesus died, he was raised from the dead. Forty days later he returned to his Father in heaven, and Mary and the disciples returned to Jerusalem. They went to a home and waited there for the coming of the Holy Spirit.

Pretend you are with Mary and the disciples in Jerusalem. In the flames write or draw what you might do while you are there.

Reading the Word of God

The Spirit Comes on Pentecost

The Holy Spirit came to the disciples on the Jewish feast of **Pentecost.** The word *pentecost* means "fifty days." The Holy Spirit came to Mary and the disciples fifty days after Jesus' Resurrection. This is what the New Testament tells happened.

The disciples were gathered in a house. Suddenly, a sound like a strong wind filled the room. Small flames of fire settled over each disciple's head.

Peter and the other disciples went out into the street. Peter told everyone about Jesus. Many people became followers of Jesus that day.

Based on Acts of the Apostles 2:1–4, 14, 41

The Holy Spirit helped the disciples teach the people about Jesus. The Holy Spirit helped the people believe in Jesus.

Name three qualities you have that would help you tell other people about Jesus.

Understanding the Word of God

The Holy Spirit Is with Us

Jesus promised that we would never be alone. We trust Jesus. We believe that the Holy Spirit is always with us.

The Church gives the Holy Spirit other names. Each name tells us something that we believe about the Holy Spirit.

Advocate. An advocate speaks for another person. An advocate also defends people. The Holy Spirit is our advocate who speaks for us to God. The Holy Spirit defends us against danger and evil. Another word for advocate is *paraclete*.

Helper. A helper assists other people who need aid to understand or do something. The Holy Spirit helps us understand and live what Jesus taught.

Guide. A guide shows us the way. The Holy Spirit shows us the way to make good decisions to live as followers of Jesus.

The Holy Spirit helps us know, love, and serve God and our neighbor. The Holy Spirit is the Advocate, Helper, and Guide who is always with us.

_____

_____

_____

_____

_____

_____

_____

_____

Amen.

Write a prayer to the Holy Spirit. Use the names of the Holy Spirit in your prayer.

Signs of the Holy Spirit

Every time we pray, the Holy Spirit moves our hearts to pray. The Church prays to the Holy Spirit. We ask the Holy Spirit to help us understand what Jesus taught and to live as Jesus' followers.

There are twelve signs that show the Holy Spirit is working in the Church. We call these the fruits of the Holy Spirit. The Holy Spirit helps us build a world with these qualities.

Our Catholic Faith

Fruits of the Holy Spirit

The fruits of the Holy Spirit are love, joy, peace, patience, kindness, goodness, generosity, gentleness, faithfulness, modesty, self-control, and chastity.

Look at each picture. On the line under each picture write the fruit of the Holy Spirit that is being used.

_____

_____

_____

_____

The Catholic Church

We belong to the Catholic Church. The Catholic Church goes all the way back to Jesus and the Apostles. The Catholic Church is made up of the pope and other bishops, priests, deacons, religious brothers and religious sisters, married and unmarried laypeople.

We become members of the Church through Baptism. At Baptism we receive the gift of sanctifying grace. The word *sanctifying* means "making holy." Sanctifying grace is the gift of God sharing his life with us. We become the holy People of God.

Everyone who belongs to the Catholic Church is part of the People of God. In the Church different people have different responsibilities and gifts. We all help others come to know Jesus and the good news of God's love for all people.

Create a headline for the front page of the newspaper The Church Today. Tell one way your parish is living as the community of God's holy people.

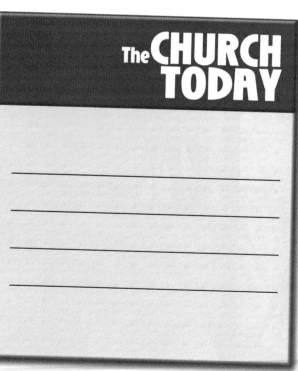

The **CHURCH TODAY**

_____

_____

_____

Our Catholic Faith

Works of Mercy

The Corporal Works of Mercy and the Spiritual Works of Mercy guide the Church in living as God's holy people. These works guide us in helping people care for the needs of their body and their soul.

The Church Today

The Catholic Church is a worldwide community of believers in Jesus Christ. A local church, or the church in a particular place, is called a diocese. A diocese has many parish churches and is led by a bishop.

All those who belong to a diocese help one another live the Gospel. Being active members of the Church enables us to be faithful followers of Jesus Christ. The way we act, the things we say, and even our attitudes show our love for God and people. The Church today helps us live as Jesus taught. When we live as a follower of Jesus, we build a kind, just, and peaceful world.

Name some of the people who help you live the Gospel.

TOYS FOR CHARITY
703

73

What Difference Does Faith Make in My Life?

At Baptism you were joined to Christ. You became a member of the Church. You are holy and belong to the holy People of God.

Write or draw how you can follow Jesus by living a holy life.

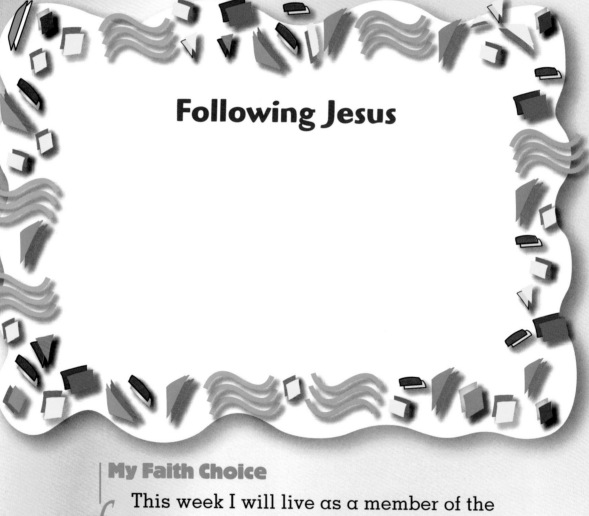

Following Jesus

My Faith Choice

This week I will live as a member of the holy People of God. I will

_____

_____ .

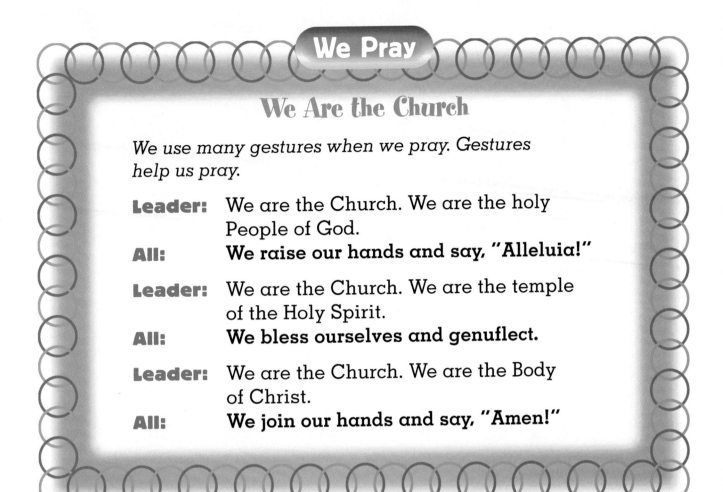

We Pray

We Are the Church

We use many gestures when we pray. Gestures help us pray.

Leader: We are the Church. We are the holy People of God.

All: **We raise our hands and say, "Alleluia!"**

Leader: We are the Church. We are the temple of the Holy Spirit.

All: **We bless ourselves and genuflect.**

Leader: We are the Church. We are the Body of Christ.

All: **We join our hands and say, "Amen!"**

We Remember

Find out the hidden message about the Church. Circle the first letter and then circle every other letter. Share the message with a friend.

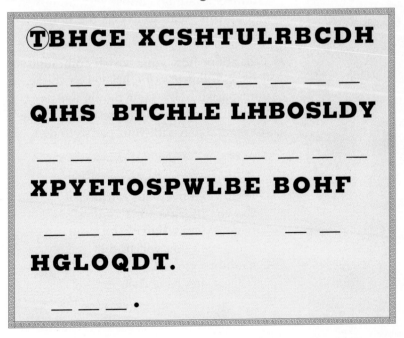

Ⓣ B H C E   X C S H T U L R B C D H

_ _ _   _ _ _ _ _ _

Q I H S   B T C H L E   L H B O S L D Y

_ _ _   _ _ _ _ _   _ _ _ _

X P Y E T O S P W L B E   B O H F

_ _ _ _ _ _   _ _ _

H G L O Q D T .

_ _ _ _ .

To Help You Remember

1. The work of the Church is to help all people come to know Jesus and invite people to be followers of Jesus.

2. All the people of the Church help others come to know Jesus.

3. All the people of the Church live holy lives.

This Week . . .

In chapter 8, "We Are the Church," your child discovered more about the Catholic Church. The Catholic Church goes back to Jesus and the Apostles. Jesus is the Head of the Church. The Church is the Body of Christ. The Church is holy; it is the holy People of God. The Church is the temple of the Holy Spirit. The Holy Spirit is present within each of us and with the whole community of the Church. The Holy Spirit gives the Church the grace to live as the holy People of God.

For more on the teachings of the Catholic Church on the mystery of the Church, see *Catechism of the Catholic Church* paragraph numbers 668–679.

Sharing God's Word

Read together the Bible story in Matthew 28:19–20 about what Jesus told the disciples after the Resurrection or read the adaptation of the story on page 70. Emphasize the responsibility the Church has today to continue the work Jesus gave to the disciples.

Praying

In this chapter your child used different gestures for prayer. Read and pray together the prayer on page 75.

Making a Difference

Choose one of the following activities to do as a family or design a similar activity of your own.

• Jesus told the disciples to share the Good News with others. Talk about how your family can share the Good News with others.

• At Baptism we receive the gift of the Holy Spirit. We are made holy and become members of the holy People of God. As a family, choose one thing you can do this week to live as the holy People of God.

• Talk about how your parish community lives as followers of Christ. List the ways your parish helps your family live as followers of Jesus. Choose one of those things and join with your parish to do it.

For more ideas on ways your family can live your faith, visit the "Faith First for Families" page at **www.FaithFirst.com**. This week you will find it useful to look at "Questions Kids Ask."

Paul the Apostle
A Scripture Story

We Pray

I will praise you,
LORD, with all
my heart.   Psalm 9:2

**God our Father,
help us tell others
about your Son,
Jesus, each day.
        Amen.**

*When have you ever
changed your mind
about something?*

Each day we learn
new things. Learning
new things helps us
change the way to do
things. Paul changed
his entire life and
became a follower of
Jesus.

*What do you know
about Saint Paul?*

Saint Paul the Apostle

Bible Background

Faith Focus

Who was Paul the Apostle?

Faith Words

Law of Moses
The Law of Moses is the Ten Commandments plus other important laws that guide the Jewish people in living the Covenant.

Saul Loved God and God's Law

Saul was a Pharisee. He became a follower of Jesus and one of the Apostles. The Pharisees were a group of Jewish people who lived the **Law of Moses** very strictly. The Law of Moses included the Ten Commandments and other laws that guided the Jewish people in living the Covenant.

Saul heard all about Jesus and his teachings. He knew about Jesus' death and his Resurrection. After the Risen Jesus returned to his Father, Saul heard what the Apostles of Jesus were teaching. This upset Saul because he thought Jesus' Apostles were speaking against the Law of Moses.

Pretend you are Saul. What question would you ask the followers of Jesus?

_____

_____ ?

Jesus Calls Saul to Be an Apostle

One day Saul and some of his friends were traveling to the city of Damascus. They wanted to arrest the disciples of the Lord, bring them back to Jerusalem, and put them on trial. This is what happened next.

Suddenly, a great light shone around Saul, he was blinded, and he fell to the ground.

Saul heard a voice say, "Saul, why are you hurting me?" Saul asked, "Who are you?" The voice said, "I am Jesus. When you hurt my followers, you hurt me. Get up and go into Damascus."

When Saul and his friends arrived in the city of Damascus, Ananias, a follower of Jesus, came to Saul. Saul was baptized and became a follower of Jesus.

Based on Acts of the Apostles 9:3–6, 8, 17–18

Saul then became known as Paul. He became an Apostle and soon began to preach and teach all about Jesus.

Discuss how you think Saul felt when he first heard the voice of Jesus speak to him.

Paul's Faith

Jesus, the Son of God, called Saul to change and grow. Paul's heart was changed. He came to believe that Jesus was the fulfillment of all God's promises. We call this the conversion of Saint Paul.

Beginning on the road to Damascus, Jesus invited Paul to come out of darkness and see with the eyes of faith. That is how faith is. It is like a seed planted in dark ground. The seed grows through the darkness. Suddenly, it breaks through the earth into the light. The sun's light feeds the seed. The seed changes and grows.

Choose a partner. Imagine that you are with Paul the Apostle. You are visiting a town to tell people about Jesus. Write what Paul might be saying to the people.

Preaching the Gospel

_____

_____

_____

_____

_____

_____

_____

Our Church Makes a Difference

Saint John Neumann

Like Paul the Apostle, many Christians have traveled and preached the Good News of Jesus. John Neumann left his home in Europe and traveled across the Atlantic Ocean to New York. He became a priest and traveled to Maryland, Virginia, Pennsylvania, and Ohio, where he preached the Gospel.

Father John Neumann became an American citizen on February 10, 1848, and the bishop of Philadelphia on March 28, 1852. He built fifty churches and opened almost one hundred Catholic schools. He wrote newspaper articles and two catechisms. John Neumann was the first American bishop to be named a saint.

Describe ways your parish shares the Good News of Jesus with others. Clue: Look for the answer in your parish Sunday bulletin.

Saint Vincent de Paul Church, Philadelphia, 1851

Our Catholic Faith

Missionaries

Saint John Neumann was a missionary. Christian missionaries often travel to a country different than their own to teach about Jesus. Bishops, priests, deacons, religious brothers and sisters, and laypeople serve the Church as missionaries.

John Neumann, bishop of Philadelphia

With My Family

This Week . . .

In chapter 9, "Paul the Apostle: A Scripture Story," your child was introduced to Paul the Apostle. Before he used his Roman name Paul, he was known as Saul. Saul was a Pharisee who loved God and lived the Law of Moses with his whole heart and strength. When Saul was traveling to Damascus, Jesus spoke to him, asking, "Why do you persecute me?" This experience began Saul's conversion from being a persecutor of Christians to living and dying as a great Apostle. Paul came to understand that Jesus and his followers are one.

For more on the teachings of the Catholic Church on the mystery of the Church, see *Catechism of the Catholic Church* paragraph numbers 737–741, 787–795, and 813–865.

Sharing God's Word

Read together the Bible story in Acts 9:1–20 about Jesus calling Saul to be his disciple or read the adaptation of the story on page 79. Emphasize that Paul became an Apostle and told others about Jesus with his whole heart and strength.

Praying

In this chapter your child prayed one of the memorial acclamations we pray at Mass. Read and pray together the acclamation on page 83.

Making a Difference

Choose one of the following activities to do as a family or design a similar activity of your own.

- Draw pictures that illustrate the Bible story about how Saul the Pharisee became known as Paul the Apostle. Display the pictures where they can serve as a reminder of the importance of teaching others about Jesus.

- Use the memorial acclamation your parish sings or prays aloud this week for your family prayer.

- When you take part in Mass this week, bring home the parish bulletin. Look through the bulletin to discover the many ways your parish shares the Good News of Jesus.

For more ideas on ways your family can live your faith, visit the "Faith First for Families" page at **www.FaithFirst.com**. Check out "Bible Stories." Read and discuss the Bible story as a family this week.

The Communion of Saints

We Pray

People who seek to
see the face of God
shall receive a
blessing from God.
Based on Psalm 24:5–6

**God our Father,
may the Holy
Spirit who blessed
the lives of the
saints bless our
lives.   Amen.**

*Who is one of your
heroes? Why?*

*Our world has many
heroes. The Church
has heroes too.*

*Who are some of the
heroes of the Church?*

Christ reaching out
to all people

The Saints of the Church

Faith Focus

Why do we call the Church the Communion of Saints?

Faith Words

saints
The saints are people whose love for God is stronger than their love for anyone or anything else.

Communion of Saints
The Communion of Saints is the community of the faithful followers of Jesus, both those living on earth and those who have died.

Heroes of the Faith

The Church honors its heroes, the **saints,** for their holiness. Saints are people whose love for God is stronger than their love for anyone or anything else. Mary, the mother of Jesus, is our most holy saint.

From their place in heaven, the saints pray for us. They offer us guidance. They protect us. We too will live with God and all the saints forever.

One way the Church honors the saints is to set aside special days to celebrate their lives. These days are called the feast days of the saints. By honoring the saints, the Church helps us remember what it means to live as children of God. Whenever we live and love as Jesus taught us, we are living holy lives. We are living as saints.

Name the one day each year the Church honors all the saints in heaven. Describe how your parish celebrates that feast day.

The Communion of Saints

In the Apostles' Creed we pray, "I believe in the **Communion of Saints.**" The Communion of Saints is made up of people living on earth who are trying to live holy lives. It also includes all the holy people who have died and are living in heaven. We honor all the saints in heaven on All Saints' Day.

Some people die and are not ready to receive the gift of heaven. They are still growing in their love for God. These people also belong to the Communion of Saints. On All Souls' Day the whole Church prays that God will welcome these people into heaven. Heaven is living in happiness with God forever.

We pray to the saints who live with God in heaven. This shows we believe that they have new life, life everlasting, as Jesus promised.

Write or draw some ways you can celebrate that you are a member of the Communion of Saints here on earth.

We Are One

Paul the Apostle called the Church the Body of Christ. Each member of the Body of Christ is an important part of the Church. Saint Paul wrote,

The Body of Christ has many parts, just as any human body does. Together we are the Body of Christ. Each of us is an important part of his Body. Based on 1 Corinthians 12:12, 27

This teaching of Saint Paul helps us understand what it means to call the Church the Communion of Saints. At Baptism we are joined to Christ and become members of the Church, the Body of Christ. We belong to the Communion of Saints. When we receive the Body and Blood of Christ in Holy Communion, we are joined most fully to Jesus and to the whole Communion of Saints.

Name one gift you have. Tell how you can use it to work with other members of the Church.

Gift	How I Can Use It

Our Lady of Guadalupe

The Church celebrates many feast days in honor of Mary. One of these is the feast of Our Lady of Guadalupe on December 12. On this feast we remember the story of Saint Juan Diego. We remember that Juan Diego spoke with a beautiful Aztec woman who told him she was Mary, the Mother of God. Mary's appearance to Juan Diego helps us believe that God's love is for everyone. People of every race and language are loved by God.

We honor Mary, Our Lady of Guadalupe, as the patron of the Americas. She prays in heaven for the people of North America and South America. We ask Mary to help us love all people and to live as the holy People of God.

Tell how the story of Saint Juan Diego and Our Lady of Guadalupe helps us treat all people with respect.

Our Catholic Faith

Holy People of God

The Church Jesus gave us is one, holy, catholic, and apostolic. These are the four marks, or essential qualities, of the Church Jesus gave us. The Church is holy because Jesus, the Holy One of God, is the Head of his Body, the Church.

Saint Juan Diego and Mary

89

What Difference Does Faith Make in My Life?

You belong to the Communion of Saints. Following the example of the saints can help you live as a saint.

Read more about Saint Charles Lwanga or about another saint. Tell what the life of the saint teaches you about living your faith in Jesus Christ.

Saint Charles Lwanga

Charles Lwanga and his friends lived in the country of Uganda in Africa. They worked for a king who treated the people harshly. Charles and his friends learned about Jesus from missionaries working in their country. They asked to be baptized and became followers of Jesus Christ.

When the king forced the missionaries to leave the country, Charles began to teach others about Jesus. The king became angry and gave the order to have Charles and his friends killed.

Charles and his friends are martyrs of the Church. That means that they died for their faith. He is the patron saint of African youth and of all young people. We celebrate the feast day of Saint Charles and his friends on June 3.

My Faith Choice

This week I will learn more about a saint. The saint I will learn more about is

_____.

Prayer of Intercession

Prayers of intercession ask God to help other people.

Leader: Let us pray to God, our loving Father, who called us to be his Church. For all the members of the Church on earth,

All: **Lord, hear our prayer.**

Leader: For all the members of the Church who have died and are waiting to be welcomed into heaven,

All: **Lord, hear our prayer.**

We Remember

Circle True under the true statements. Circle False under the false statements. Make the false statements true.

1. The saints are examples for us to follow.
True   False

2. The saints pray for us.
True   False

3. We pray for the saints.
True   False

To Help You Remember

1. Saints are people whose love for God is stronger than their love for anyone or anything else.

2. The Communion of Saints is made up of holy people living on earth and those who have died.

3. The Church is the Body of Christ, the Holy One of God.

This Week . . .

In chapter 10, "The Communion of Saints," your child learned that the Church is the Communion of Saints. The Communion of Saints is made up of those people living on earth, the faithful who have died and who have received the gift of heaven, and those faithful who have died who are not ready to receive the gift of heaven and are waiting to receive the gift of everlasting happiness. The Church honors the saints in heaven as heroes of our faith. Their lives are examples of how we can live a holy life as members of the Body of Christ, the Church. Sharing in the Eucharist unites us more closely with Jesus and the whole Communion of Saints and gives us the strength to live as a saint.

For more on the teachings of the Catholic Church on the mysteries of the Communion of Saints and everlasting life, see *Catechism of the Catholic Church* paragraph numbers 946–959, 1172–1173, and 1402–1405.

Sharing God's Word

Read together the Bible story in 1 Corinthians 12:12–13, 27 about what Paul the Apostle wrote about the Church or read the adaptation of the passage on page 88. Emphasize that Paul taught that every member of the Church is important.

Praying

In this chapter your child prayed a prayer of intercession. Read and pray together the prayer on page 91.

Making a Difference

Choose one of the following activities to do as a family or design a similar activity of your own.

- Find out more about Saint Juan Diego and Our Lady of Guadalupe. Read a children's book about Juan Diego to help you share more of this wonderful story together.

- Talk about the talents each member of your family has. As a family, choose one thing you can do this week to continue the work of Christ.

- Take some time this week to find out more about the patron saint of your parish or a saint who is special to your family. Visit www.FaithFirst.com or look in your public or parish library.

For more ideas on ways your family can live your faith, visit the "Faith First for Families" page at **www.FaithFirst.com**. Click on the "Saints" page and discover ways your family can live as followers of Jesus.

A. The Best Word or Phrase

Complete the sentences. Circle the best choice under each sentence.

1. The gift of _____ helps us believe in God.
   a. love   b. hope   c. faith

2. The _____ is the mystery of one God in three Persons.
   a. Holy Trinity   b. Holy Family   c. Holy Spirit

3. God's love and care for creation is called _____ .
   a. divine Providence b. divine joy   c. stewardship

4. The _____ is the announcement to Mary that God chose her to be the mother of Jesus.
   a. Resurrection   b. Annunciation   c. Nativity

5. Jesus is called the _____ because he is the Anointed One of God who saves us from our sins.
   a. Son of God   b. Messiah   c. Christ the King

6. The _____ is the name for Jesus' Passion, death, Resurrection, and Ascension.
   a. Paschal Mystery   b. Crucifixion   c. Incarnation

7. The Holy Spirit came to the disciples on the Jewish feast of _____ .
   a. Pentecost   b. Easter   c. Passover

8. The Communion of _____ includes all the faithful followers of Jesus, including those on earth today and those who have died.
   a. Apostles   b. Bishops   c. Saints

B. Jesus and the Holy Spirit

Circle the † next to the words that tell about Jesus.
Circle the 🕊 next to the words that tell about the
Holy Spirit.

† 🕊 Messiah   † 🕊 Helper   † 🕊 Advocate

† 🕊 Savior   † 🕊 Guide   † 🕊 Son of God

C. What I Have Learned

1. What are two new things you learned in this unit?

_____

_____

2. Look back at the list of faith words on page 12.
   Circle the words you now know. Tell your group the
   meaning of two of the words.

D. From a Scripture Story

The story of Pentecost has a cause and an effect.
Write the effect of the story in the chart.

Cause	Effect
The Holy Spirit comes to the disciples.	_____ _____ _____ _____ _____

What are some times the Church celebrates as a community?

Getting Ready

What I Have Learned

What is something you already know about these faith words?

Paschal Mystery

_____

_____

The liturgical year

_____

_____

The Eucharist

_____

_____

Words to Know

Put an X next to the faith words you know. Put a ? next to the faith words you need to know more about.

Faith Words

_____ liturgy

_____ Eucharist

_____ Blessed Sacrament

_____ parable

_____ Reconciliation

_____ Holy Orders

Questions I Have

What questions would you like to ask about the Eucharist?

_____

_____

A Scripture Story

Wedding in Cana

What did Jesus do at the wedding in Cana?

The Church's Year

We Pray

With all my heart
    I praise the LORD,
    our God.
        Based on Psalm 111:1

**Father, always
and everywhere
we give you
thanks through
Jesus Christ,
your Son.   Amen.**

*What days do you
and your family like
to celebrate?*

Celebrating special
times is fun. The
Church celebrates
too. We gather to
celebrate our faith in
Christ.

*What are your
favorite celebrations
of the Church?*

Faith Focus

How does the Church celebrate its faith in Jesus Christ throughout the year?

Faith Words

worship

Worship is the adoration and honor we give to God.

liturgy

The liturgy is the Church's work of worshiping God.

The Liturgical Year

The Church gathers all year long to celebrate its faith in Jesus Christ. We gather to **worship** God. We call this work of the Church the **liturgy.**

The Church's year of worship is called the liturgical year. The liturgical year is made up of the seasons of Advent, Christmas, Lent, Easter, and Ordinary Time.

Advent and Christmas

Advent begins the liturgical year. We prepare for Christmas. We wait in hope for Christ's return in glory at the end of time. During Christmas we praise and thank God for sending us Jesus, the Savior of the world.

Share with a partner how you like to celebrate Advent and Christmas.

Lent and Easter

During Lent we prepare for Easter. We join with those preparing for Baptism. We prepare to renew the promises we made at our Baptism. At the conclusion of Lent during Holy Week, the Church celebrates the Easter Triduum. The Easter Triduum is the center of the liturgical year. The word *triduum* means "three days."

The Easter Triduum begins on Holy Thursday evening and ends on Easter Sunday evening. It includes the celebrations on Holy Thursday, Good Friday, and the Easter Vigil/Easter Sunday. During these three days we celebrate and share in Jesus' Passion, death, and Resurrection.

The fifty days of the Easter season are celebrated next. During Easter we celebrate and remember Jesus' Resurrection and Ascension. The remaining weeks of the liturgical year are called Ordinary Time.

Faith-Filled People

The Elect

At the Easter Vigil you may see a special group of people. They are called the Elect. They have accepted God's invitation to become members of the Church. At the Easter Vigil they receive the sacraments of Baptism, Confirmation, and Eucharist.

Look at the four pictures. On the lines write the Church season each shows.

Ordinary Time

Ordinary Time is the longest part of the liturgical year. Ordinary Time includes the weeks that are not part of the seasons of Advent, Christmas, Lent, or Easter.

There are two parts of Ordinary Time. The first part begins after Christmas and continues to Lent. The second part begins after the fifty days of the Easter season and continues to Advent.

During Ordinary Time we listen to stories from the Gospels that tell us about Jesus' life and his saving work while he was on earth. We come to know Jesus more and more. We learn how we can live as his followers.

On the line write the title of one of your favorite Gospel stories. Draw or write something from the story in the space.

My Favorite Gospel Story

_____

Feasts of the Lord

All throughout the liturgical year we celebrate the faith of the Church in Jesus Christ. In addition to Christmas and the saving events of Jesus' Passion, death, Resurrection, and Ascension, the Church celebrates other feasts of the Lord.

Epiphany

Baptism of the Lord

Annunciation

Transfiguration

Presentation of the Lord

These feasts of the Lord remember and proclaim that Jesus is the Son of God and Savior of the world. He is the new and everlasting Covenant of friendship that God has made with all people.

Christ the King

Talk about how celebrating these six feasts can help you grow in your faith in Jesus Christ.

What Difference Does Faith Make in My Life?

The Church's liturgical year helps you keep your faith alive. When you take part in the celebrations of the liturgical year, you share in God's love.

Describe how the liturgical season the Church is celebrating now helps you live as a follower of Jesus.

Living as a Follower of Jesus

The Church is now celebrating the season of

_____.

During this season I will remember that Jesus

_____.

I will try to follow Jesus by _____

_____.

My Faith Choice

This week I will celebrate that I am a follower of Jesus. I will

_____

_____.

Thank You, God

Learn to sign this prayer of thanksgiving. Pray it alone and with other people.

Thank you,   God,   for   everything.

We Remember

Use the clues to complete the puzzle.

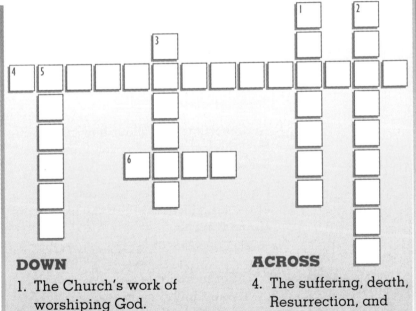

DOWN

1. The Church's work of worshiping God.
2. We celebrate Jesus, the Son of God, coming to us as the Savior of the world.
3. We celebrate Jesus' being raised from the dead.
5. We prepare for Christmas.

ACROSS

4. The suffering, death, Resurrection, and Ascension of Jesus.
6. We get ready for Easter.

To Help You Remember

1. The Church's year of worship is called the liturgical year. The seasons of the liturgical year are Advent, Christmas, Lent, Easter, and Ordinary Time.

2. The center of the liturgical year is the Easter Triduum.

3. Ordinary Time is the longest part of the liturgical year.

This Week . . .

In chapter 11, "The Church's Year," your child learned about the Church's year of worship, or the liturgical year. Like the calendar year, the liturgical year is made up of a cycle of seasons and important days. The Easter Triduum, or the three days of Holy Thursday, Good Friday, and Easter Vigil/Easter Sunday, is the heart of the liturgical year. The seasons of Advent, Christmas, Lent, and Easter revolve around this solemn three-day celebration of Christ's Passion, death, and Resurrection. The remaining weeks of the liturgical year are called Ordinary Time.

For more on the teachings of the Catholic Church on the liturgy and the liturgical year, see *Catechism of the Catholic Church* paragraph numbers 1135–1186.

Sharing God's Word

Reread the Gospel passage that you heard proclaimed at Mass this week. You can find the reading by clicking "Gospel Reflection" at www.FaithFirst.com. Emphasize how the reading helps you grow and live your faith in Jesus Christ.

Praying

In this chapter your child learned to sign a short thanksgiving prayer. Ask your child to teach you the prayer on page 103. Pray the prayer together.

Making a Difference

Choose one of the following activities to do as a family or design a similar activity of your own.

- When you take part in Mass this weekend, look at the color of the vestments and identify what liturgical season it is. Look around the church for other clues that tell you about the liturgical season.

- At dinnertime talk about how celebrating the liturgical year helps you grow in and live your faith in Jesus Christ.

- Create place mats for the current season of the liturgical year. Use the place mats at family meals.

For more ideas on ways your family can live your faith, visit the "Faith First for Families" page at **www.FaithFirst.com**. This week take time to read an article from "Just for Parents."

Celebrations of God's Love

We Pray

Sing to God with
hearts full of
happiness and joy;
praise God and give
him glory.
Based on Psalm 66:1–2

**Father, you give
us grace through
the sacraments.
Help us live as
signs of your love
for all people.
Amen.**

*What makes family
celebrations special?*

Families celebrate
special family
times. Our Church
family celebrates
the sacraments to
remember and share
in God's love.

*What sacraments
have you celebrated?*

Baptism of an infant

We Celebrate the Sacraments

Faith Focus

What do the sacraments do that brings us closer to Jesus?

Faith Words

sacraments
The sacraments are the seven special signs that make Jesus present to us and make us sharers in the life of the Holy Trinity.

Sacraments of Initiation
Baptism, Confirmation, and Eucharist are the Sacraments of Initiation.

On the top line write the name of one sacrament you have received. On the other lines write one thing about the sacrament.

Jesus Gives Us the Sacraments

Our Church celebrates the **sacraments.** There are seven sacraments. They are Baptism, Confirmation, Eucharist, Anointing of the Sick, Penance, Holy Orders, and Matrimony.

Jesus gave us the sacraments. The sacraments make us sharers in the life of the Holy Trinity. God the Father invites us to give him praise and thanksgiving. Jesus helps us bring the good news of God's love to others. The Holy Spirit helps us become more like Jesus.

Baptism

Baptism is one of the three **Sacraments of Initiation.** They are Baptism, Confirmation, and the Eucharist. Baptism is the first sacrament we receive. If we are baptized as an infant, our parents and godparents, or sponsors, ask the Church to baptize us. Our godparents promise to help our parents teach us about Jesus and how to live as Jesus taught.

The priest, or deacon, uses water to baptize us. Through Baptism we are joined to Christ. We receive new life in Christ and are born into the Church family. Our sins are forgiven, and we receive the gift of the Holy Spirit.

Pouring water to baptize

In Baptism, we are marked with a lasting sign, or character. We are followers of Christ forever. That is why we can be baptized only one time.

Ask your family about your Baptism. If your family has your baptismal candle, use it at mealtime prayers this week.

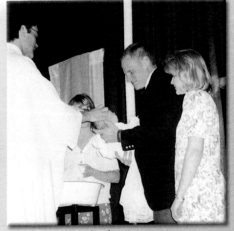
Anointing with chrism

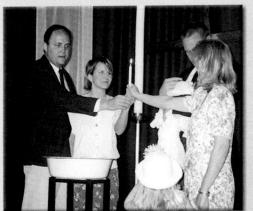
Receiving a lighted baptismal candle

Confirmation

Confirmation completes and strengthens us to live our Baptism. Like Baptism, we can only receive this sacrament one time. In Confirmation, we are also marked with a permanent sign, or character.

Confirmation usually takes place at Mass. After the Gospel reading, the bishop, or the priest chosen by him, asks the candidates for Confirmation to renew their baptismal promises. He then extends his hands over all the candidates and prays, "Send your Spirit upon them to be their Helper and Guide."

Our sponsor, who can be one of our godparents, presents us to the bishop. The bishop lays his hand on our head and anoints us with the blessed oil of chrism, saying, "*(Name)*, be sealed with the Gift of the Holy Spirit." The Holy Spirit strengthens us to bring Jesus to the world.

Write a question about Confirmation. This week try to find the answer to your question.

We Are Blessed by God

All believers ask for God's blessing. We ask God to be with us in all we say and do. Blessings of people, meals, objects, and places are sacramentals of the Church. Sacramentals are objects and blessings that we use in our worship and prayer.

Holy water, blessed oils, the crucifix, and blessed religious medals are sacramentals. The ashes we receive on our foreheads on Ash Wednesday are examples of objects that are sacramentals.

The Church asks for God's blessing in the name of Christ while making the sign of the cross of Christ. This shows that in Christ we are blessed by God the Father, God the Son, and God the Holy Spirit.

Our Catholic Faith

Holy Water

Water is one of the main sacramentals of the Church. Water reminds us that God is the giver of all life. He gives us the gift of life on earth and of eternal life in heaven.

What sacramentals do you use? Tell how they help you pray.

What Difference Does Faith Make in My Life?

You are a sign of God's love. By celebrating the sacraments you grow closer to God the Father, Jesus, and the Holy Spirit. You receive the grace to help others grow in their love for God.

Write a letter to a friend. Explain how one of the sacraments that you have received helps you live as a follower of Jesus.

My Faith Choice

This week I will show that I am a follower of Jesus Christ. I will

_____

_____.

A Prayer of Meditation

A meditation is a prayer in which we use our imagination. Follow these directions and pray a prayer of meditation.

1. Close your eyes. Remember that the Holy Spirit lives within you.

2. Pretend you are sitting among a group of people on a mountainside listening to Jesus.

3. Listen as a reader reads Matthew 5:14–16.

4. Ask the Holy Spirit to help you learn how to be a light in the world.

5. Make a decision to live as a follower of Jesus.

We Remember

Use the code to discover a message about the sacraments.

A	B	C	D	E	F	G	H	I	J	K	L	M
1	2	3	4	5	6	7	8	9	10	11	12	13

N	O	P	Q	R	S	T	U	V	W	X	Y	Z
14	15	16	17	18	19	20	21	22	23	24	25	26

19 1 3 18 1 13 5 14 20 19

13 1 11 5   21 19

19 8 1 18 5 18 19   9 14

7 15 4 19   12 9 6 5

1 14 4   12 15 22 5

To Help You Remember

1. The sacraments make Jesus present to us in a special way.

2. Baptism joins us to Christ and to the Body of Christ, the Church.

3. Confirmation strengthens our Baptism and helps us live as Jesus' followers.

This Week . . .

In chapter 12, "Celebrations of God's Love," your child learned about the sacraments. In particular your child explored the meaning of the celebration of Baptism and Confirmation. Jesus gave us the gift of the seven sacraments. Through taking part in the celebration of the sacraments we join with Christ and are made sharers in the very life of God—Father, Son, and Holy Spirit. Joined to Christ through Baptism and strengthened by the gift of the Holy Spirit, we give praise to the Father through a life of holiness.

For more on the teachings of the Catholic Church on the sacraments in general and on the sacraments of Baptism and Confirmation, see *Catechism of the Catholic Church* paragraph numbers 1135–1158, 1210–1211, 1212–1274, and 1285–1314.

Sharing God's Word

Read together the Gospel story in Matthew 28:16–20 about Jesus sending the disciples to baptize people. Emphasize that the sacrament of Baptism joins us to Christ and to the Body of Christ, the Church.

Praying

In this chapter your child prayed a prayer of meditation. Read and pray together the prayer on page 111.

Making a Difference

Choose one of the following activities to do as a family or design a similar activity of your own.

- Write the names of each of the seven sacraments on separate index cards. Have a member of the family choose a card and talk about why that sacrament is important to the Church. Continue until all the cards have been chosen.

- Find photos and other mementos of each family member's celebration of Baptism. One by one talk about each family member's Baptism.

- At dinnertime talk about how using oil in cooking helps prepare foods for meals. Then talk about how anointing in Baptism is a sign that the Holy Spirit helps us live as followers of Jesus.

For more ideas on ways your family can live your faith, visit the "Faith First for Families" page at **www.FaithFirst.com**. You're only a click away from taking a "Tour of a Church" with your child.

We Celebrate the Eucharist

Wheat and bread, symbols for the Eucharist

We Pray

LORD, our God, it is
good to give you
thanks all day long.
Based on Psalm 92:2–3

**Father,
all-powerful and
ever-living God,
we do well always
and everywhere
to give you thanks
through Jesus
Christ our Lord.
Amen.**

*What important meals
have you eaten with
your family?*

Sharing a meal
strengthens the love
of family members for
one another. The most
important celebration
of the Church is the
Eucharist.

*What do we celebrate
at the Eucharist?*

113

We Give Thanks to God

Faith Focus

What do we celebrate at the Eucharist?

Faith Words

Eucharist
The Eucharist is the sacrament in which the Church gives thanks to God and shares in the Body and Blood of Christ.

Blessed Sacrament
The Blessed Sacrament is a name given to the Eucharist, the real presence of the Body and Blood of Jesus under the forms of bread and wine.

Jesus Shares a Special Meal

On the night before he died, Jesus shared his last meal with his disciples. We call this meal the Last Supper, or the Lord's Supper. This is what happened.

Jesus took bread, prayed a special blessing prayer, and broke the bread. He gave the bread to his disciples, saying, "Take and eat this. This is my body."

Then Jesus took a cup of wine and gave thanks to his Father. He gave the wine to his disciples, saying, "Drink from this cup, all of you, for this is my blood." Based on Matthew 26:26–28

The Church does what Jesus did at the Last Supper when we celebrate the Eucharist. We join with Jesus. We give thanks to God the Father. We share the Body and Blood of Jesus.

Talk about the first time you received the Body and Blood of Christ.

We Give Thanks

The Church celebrates the Eucharist at Mass. The Sunday celebration of the **Eucharist** is at the heart of our life as Catholics. The word *eucharist* means "to give thanks." Catholics have a serious duty, or obligation, to participate in the celebration of the Mass on Sundays.

The Liturgy of the Word is the first main part of the Mass. God is present with us. He speaks to us through the readings from Sacred Scripture.

The Liturgy of the Eucharist is the second main part of the Mass. The Church does what Jesus did at the Last Supper. We join with Jesus in offering himself to God. We remember and share in Jesus' life, Passion, death, and Resurrection. The bread and wine become the Body and Blood of Christ. We receive the gift of the Body and Blood of Christ in Holy Communion. This joins us more fully to Jesus Christ and to all the members of his Church.

Decorate the poster.

Jesus Is the Bread of Life

The Blessed Sacrament

Sometimes there are consecrated hosts left over after the faithful have received Holy Communion at Mass. The consecrated hosts are brought to the tabernacle. The consecrated hosts are also called the **Blessed Sacrament.**

A special lighted candle is kept near the tabernacle. This candle is called the sanctuary lamp. This reminds us that the Blessed Sacrament is in the tabernacle. Jesus is truly present with us.

The Church brings the Blessed Sacrament as Holy Communion to people who are elderly, sick, or in the hospital. We also worship Jesus by praying before him present in the Blessed Sacrament.

Design a tabernacle for your church.

Holy Days of Obligation

Each year Catholics celebrate holy days of obligation that are not always celebrated on Sunday. These holy days celebrate very important events in God's plan of salvation. Catholics have the responsibility to participate in Mass on these holy days just as they do on Sundays.

There are six holy days of obligation that Catholics in the United States celebrate. They are the Solemnity of Mary, the Mother of God; the Ascension of Our Lord; the Assumption of the Blessed Virgin Mary into Heaven; All Saints; the Immaculate Conception of Mary; and Christmas Day. When we participate in Mass on these days, we help others see the difference that keeping God first in our lives makes.

Find out when the Church celebrates the six holy days of obligation this year.

Our Catholic Faith

Precepts of the Church

The Church is our teacher and guide. One way the Church guides us is by giving us precepts, or rules, that state some of our responsibilities. One of the five precepts of the Church says that Catholics are to participate in the Eucharist on Sundays and on holy days of obligation.

117

What Difference Does Faith Make in My Life?

At the end of Mass the priest dismisses the people, using these or similar words, "Go in peace to love and serve the Lord."

Check three ways you can love and serve the Lord this week. Tell a partner exactly what you could do.

Love and Serve the Lord

❒ Help at home without being asked.

❒ Pray for someone.

❒ Cheer up someone.

❒ Share my games.

❒ Say I'm sorry.

❒ Help my teacher.

My Faith Choice

This week at Mass I will take time to thank God for all his blessings to me. I will thank God for

_____

_____

Lift Up Our Hearts to God

At Mass we pray the preface. This prepares us to pray the Eucharistic Prayer. Pray this part of the preface.

Leader: Let us lift up our hearts and give thanks to God for the gift of the Eucharist.

All: Give thanks to the Lord our God. It is right to give him thanks and praise.

Group 1: Father, we give you thanks always and everywhere through Jesus Christ.

Group 2: With all the angels and saints, we give you thanks and praise.

All: Give thanks to the Lord our God. It is right to give him thanks and praise.

We Remember

Complete each sentence. Use the words in the word bank.

- -

Eucharist   Word   Last Supper

- -

1. The _____ is the meal at which Jesus gave us the Eucharist.

2. The Liturgy of the _____ is the first main part of the Mass.

3. The Liturgy of the _____ is the second main part of the Mass.

To Help You Remember

1. At the Eucharist we celebrate what Jesus did at the Last Supper.

2. At Mass we listen to the word of God and we share the Eucharist.

3. At the Eucharist the bread and wine become the Body and Blood of Christ, through the words of the priest and the power of the Holy Spirit.

This Week . . .

In chapter 13, "We Celebrate the Eucharist," your child learned more about the celebration of Mass and the mystery of the Eucharist. During the Liturgy of the Word at Mass we listen and respond to the word of God. During the Liturgy of the Eucharist we do what Jesus did at the Last Supper. We share in the Body and Blood of Christ and are made sharers in the Paschal Mystery of Jesus. After Mass the leftover consecrated bread is reserved in the tabernacle for distribution to the faithful who are sick or elderly and for the adoration of the faithful. The Blessed Sacrament is another name for the Eucharist.

For more on the teachings of the Catholic Church on the liturgical celebration of the Mass, see *Catechism of the Catholic Church* paragraph numbers 1322–1405.

Sharing God's Word

Read together the Bible story in Matthew 26:26–28 about the Last Supper or read the adaptation of this story on page 114. Emphasize that Jesus gave us the Eucharist at the Last Supper.

Praying

In this chapter your child prayed part of the preface that we pray at Mass. Read and pray together the prayer on page 119.

Making a Difference

Choose one of the following activities to do as a family or design a similar activity of your own.

- When you participate in Mass this week, join in with the assembly in praying the preface. Remember that we pray the preface to prepare for the Eucharistic Prayer.

- At the conclusion of Mass, the priest dismisses the assembly, using these or similar words, "Go in peace to love and serve the Lord." As a family, choose one thing you can do this week to love and serve the Lord.

- After you participate in Mass this week, make a visit to the Blessed Sacrament. Thank Jesus for sharing his life with us.

For more ideas on ways your family can live your faith, visit the "Faith First for Families" page at **www.FaithFirst.com**. This week share some of the family ideas on the "Gospel Reflections" page.

The Pharisee and the Tax Collector

A Scripture Story

We Pray

LORD, my God, I place
my trust in you.
Based on Psalm 25:2

God our Father,
we know that
you are good.
You love us and
do great things
for us.   Amen.

What is one of your favorite stories?

There are many stories in the Gospels that Jesus told. We listen to these at Mass.

What stories do you know that Jesus told?

The Pharisee and the tax collector praying in the Temple in Jerusalem

Bible Background

Faith Focus

Why did Jesus tell the story about the Pharisee and the tax collector?

Faith Words

parables
Parables are stories that Jesus told to help people understand and live what he was teaching.

Parables

Jesus told stories called **parables** to teach people. In these stories Jesus included people and places his listeners knew. This helped the people listening to him understand what he was teaching.

Some of the many people who listened to Jesus were Pharisees. Pharisees were religious leaders of the Jewish people. Some Pharisees believed that they were better than other people.

Tax collectors also listened to Jesus. Some tax collectors took more money than people owed. They kept the extra money for themselves. Because of this, many Jewish people thought the tax collectors were sinners and they stayed away from them.

Name two things you have learned about Pharisees and two things about tax collectors in Jesus' time.

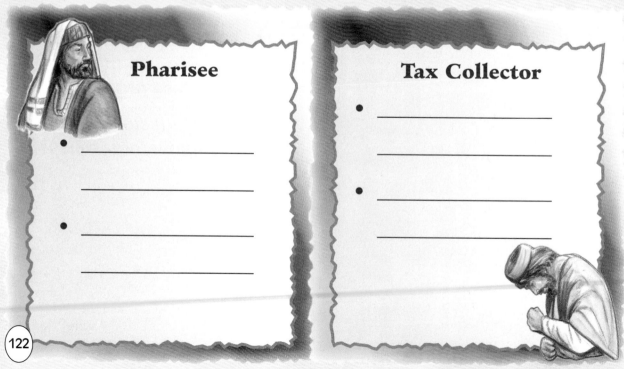

Pharisee

- _____
  _____
- _____
  _____

Tax Collector

- _____
  _____
- _____
  _____

The Pharisee and Tax Collector

One day Jesus told a parable about a Pharisee and a tax collector. Here is part of the parable Jesus told.

Two men went into the Temple in Jerusalem to pray. One was a Pharisee. The other was a tax collector. The Pharisee stood in the center of the Temple. He thanked God that he was not greedy or dishonest like other people. The tax collector stood toward the back of the Temple. He beat his chest with his hand to show he was sorry for his sins. He prayed, "God forgive me, for I am a sinner."

Based on Luke 18:10–11, 13

What prayer do you like to pray to ask God to help you live as a follower of Jesus?

God Forgives the Humble

The parable of the Pharisee and the Tax Collector teaches people that God wants people to be humble. A humble person believes that God is the giver of all gifts. Humble people also know they need God's mercy.

The tax collector in the parable is humble and honest. He knows and admits he has sinned. He knows he needs God's mercy. In deep sorrow, he trusts that God will hear his prayer and forgive him.

Everyone needs to be humble like the tax collector in the parable. Every person needs God's forgiveness and mercy. All our blessings, including God's forgiveness, are gifts from God. We humbly thank God for his great goodness and mercy to us.

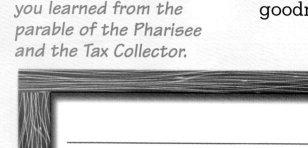

Write a four-line poem or song that tells what you learned from the parable of the Pharisee and the Tax Collector.

ST. AUGUSTINE

Saint Augustine

Many saints show us what happens when we are humble. When he was young, Augustine was very proud like the Pharisee in the parable. He felt he didn't need forgiveness from God at all.

As Augustine got older, he came to believe that he really needed and wanted God's forgiveness. For the rest of his life, he prayed often and asked for forgiveness. The Holy Spirit helped Augustine change. He became a humble and happy man.

Saint Augustine shows us what can happen when we are humble. We can show others that happiness comes from trusting God and making God first in our lives.

What does Augustine teach us about being humble and happy?

Our Catholic Faith

Prayer Gestures

Prayer gestures show that we believe and trust in God. Standing and kneeling, bowing our heads and genuflecting are four gestures we use during the liturgy. The tax collector touched his chest with his hand. This gesture showed he believed that he needed God's mercy and forgiveness.

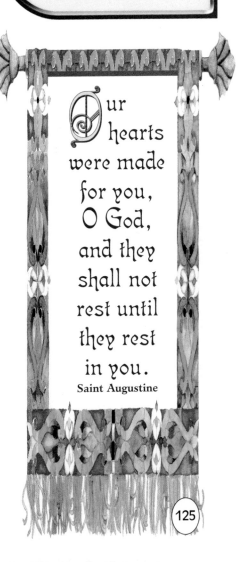

Our hearts were made for you, O God, and they shall not rest until they rest in you.
Saint Augustine

125

What Difference Does Faith Make in My Life?

Each year you are learning what a difference it makes to recognize and trust in God's forgiveness. You are learning to be humble.

Work with a partner. Create a role-play about asking for forgiveness or about forgiving others. Write your ideas here.

Forgiveness

_____

_____

_____

_____

_____

_____

_____

My Faith Choice

This week I will be a "forgiveness" person. I will

_____

_____ .

Lord, Have Mercy

We pray the "Lord, have mercy" prayer at Mass.
We show God that we are humble and need his
mercy. Pray this prayer together.

Leader: Lord, you were sent to heal those
who were sorry for their sins.

All: **Lord, have mercy.**

Leader: Lord, you came to call sinners.

All: **Christ, have mercy.**

Leader: Lord, you ask your Father to forgive us.

All: **Lord, have mercy.**

Leader: May almighty God have mercy on us,
forgive us our sins, and bring us to
everlasting life.

All: **Amen.**

We Remember

Circle the words in the puzzle that will help you
remember the parable. Use the terms to retell it.

| pray | humble | proud | Pharisee |
| tax collector | Temple | sin |

P	H	A	R	I	S	E	E	X	O	T	M	N
R	A	C	N	I	E	M	P	R	O	U	D	E
A	B	H	U	M	B	L	E	P	R	A	Y	V
T	A	X	C	O	L	L	E	C	T	O	R	I
D	R	S	I	N	P	A	B	L	I	C	Y	N
R	R	R	A	L	T	E	M	P	L	E	B	O	N

To Help You Remember

1. Jesus told parables to help his listeners understand what he was teaching.

2. The parable of the Pharisee and the Tax Collector teaches us to be humble.

3. The parable of the Pharisee and the Tax Collector teaches us that everyone needs God's forgiveness.

This Week . . .

In chapter 14, "The Pharisee and the Tax Collector: A Scripture Story," your child listened to the parable of the Pharisee and the Tax Collector. A parable usually included people and places that the teacher's listeners knew well. This helped the listeners understand the message of the story. The teacher would use the people and places in such a way that the ending of the story would sometimes come as a surprise to the listeners. This too helped the teacher emphasize the point of the parable. The message of the parable of the Pharisee and the Tax Collector tells us that everyone is in need of God's forgiveness. We need to approach God humbly and with trust. This point is made by contrasting the attitude and actions of the Pharisee with those of the tax collector.

For more on the teachings of the Catholic Church on the purpose of parables and the teaching of the parable of the Pharisee and the Tax Collector, see *Catechism of the Catholic Church* paragraph numbers 546, 2607, 2613, and 2839.

Sharing God's Word

Read together the parable in Luke 18:9–13 about the Pharisee and the tax collector or read the adaptation of the parable on page 123. Emphasize the attitude of the tax collector.

Praying

In this chapter your child prayed a prayer of mercy based on a prayer we sometimes pray at the beginning of Mass. Read and pray together the prayer on page 127.

Making a Difference

Choose one of the following activities to do as a family or design a similar activity of your own.

- At dinnertime this week use appropriate prayer gestures. Talk about how our prayer gestures reflect and give expression to our attitudes or feelings about prayer.

- Pantomime the parable presented in this chapter. Take turns acting out the roles of the Pharisee and the tax collector.

- Create and display a poster that reminds your family to be a forgiving family.

For more ideas on ways your family can live your faith, visit the "Faith First for Families" page at **www.FaithFirst.com**. Check out "Bible Stories." Read and discuss the Bible story this week.

We Celebrate God's Healing Love

We Pray

Have mercy on me,
God, in your
goodness.

Psalm 51:3

**Father,
we ask your
mercy through
Jesus Christ, your
Son, our Lord.
Amen.**

*When is a time you
needed someone to
forgive you?*

Sometimes we need
to ask God for
forgiveness. We
celebrate forgiveness
in our families and in
our Church.

*When do we
celebrate God's
forgiveness with
our Church?*

God, Our Forgiving Father

Faith Focus

How do the Sacraments of Healing help us share in God's healing love?

Faith Words

sin
Sin is freely choosing to do or say something that we know is against God's Law.

Sacraments of Healing
Reconciliation and Anointing of the Sick are the two Sacraments of Healing.

The Forgiving Father

Do you remember hearing the parable of the Forgiving Father? It is also called the parable of the Prodigal Son. In this parable the younger son of a father demands his share of the family goods and money. He leaves home and wastes all his money. Here is what happens next.

The son was very hungry and sorry for what he had done. He decided to return home and ask his father for forgiveness. As he came near his father's home, the father ran down the road to greet his son. The father forgave his son and welcomed him home.

Based on Luke 15:16–24

1 = D   2 = F   3 = G   4 = L   5 = R
6 = S   7 = V   8 = W   9 = Y

$\frac{}{3}\frac{O}{1}\ \frac{A}{4}\frac{}{8}\ \frac{A}{9}\frac{}{6}$

$\frac{O}{2}\frac{}{5}\frac{I}{3}\ \frac{E}{7}\frac{}{6}\ \frac{U}{6}.$

Use this code to discover the message of the parable of the Forgiving Father.

Reconciliation

Every day we make choices just as the son made choices in the parable of the Forgiving Father. Most of the choices we make are good choices. Sometimes we make choices that are against God's laws. We **sin.** Sin always hurts our friendship with God and with other people. When we sin, we need to ask God for forgiveness.

Because we need forgiveness, Jesus gave us the sacrament of Reconciliation. This sacrament is also called the sacrament of Penance. It is one of the two **Sacraments of Healing.**

In Reconciliation we share in God's forgiveness and mercy. We are forgiven the sins we commit after we are baptized. We confess our sins to a priest. We show God we are sorry for our sins. Through the power of the Holy Spirit and the words and actions of the priest, God forgives us and heals us with his grace. The Holy Spirit helps us not to sin again. We are reconciled, or made friends again, with God and the members of the Church.

Describe one way you can show someone you forgive them.

✗ Faith-Filled People

Peter the Apostle

Saint Peter the Apostle knew how much Jesus forgave people. Once Peter denied he was a disciple of Jesus. Peter knew Jesus forgave him by the way Jesus looked at him. Jesus gave Peter and the other Apostles the power to forgive sins in his name. The Church celebrates the feast day of Saint Peter the Apostle on June 29.

Anointing of the Sick

Jesus healed the sick during his life on earth. He healed their bodies and their souls. Jesus continues this work in a special way through the sacrament of the Anointing of the Sick. This sacrament is the second Sacrament of Healing.

When we are seriously ill or weak because of old age or in danger of dying, our Church family takes care of us. We celebrate the Anointing of the Sick. In this sacrament the Church prays for us. The Church shares God's word with us and with those who have gathered to share in the celebration. The priest anoints our hands and forehead with the oil of the sick. He prays that we will trust in God's care.

This sacrament brings us God's grace. This grace strengthens our faith and trust in God. It gives us strength and courage and peace.

Draw or write something you could do if a member of your family was sick.

The Pope Forgives

On May 13, 1981, in Saint Peter's Square in Rome, Italy, a large crowd was cheering for Pope John Paul II. A man fired two shots. The bullets hit the pope's arm, hand, and stomach. When people around the world wanted the man punished, the pope said, "Pray for the brother who shot me, whom I have sincerely forgiven."

Two years later Pope John Paul II visited the man in prison. They talked privately for twenty minutes. When the visit was over, the man leaned over and kissed the hand of the man he had tried to kill. He knew what it meant to be forgiven. Pope John Paul II was a living sign of God's mercy for the man who shot him.

What does this story teach you about the healing power of forgiveness?

Our Catholic Faith

The Merciful

Mercy brings us healing and forgiveness. In chapter 5 you learned about the Beatitudes. One of the Beatitudes tells us to be merciful to others. In this Beatitude Jesus taught us to share God's healing love with people as he did. When we do, we receive God's mercy.

What Difference Does Faith Make in My Life?

Asking and receiving forgiveness is an important part of your life. The Holy Spirit helps you bring the healing love of forgiveness to others.

Put a 1 next to the words you could use to ask forgiveness. Put a 2 next to the words you could use to forgive someone else. With a partner prepare a role-play for your class that includes these words.

Forgiveness Words

_____ "I'm sorry."

_____ "You are forgiven."

_____ "That's okay."

_____ "I'll try not to do that again."

_____ "We're still friends."

_____ "Can we be friends again?"

_____ "I know I was wrong to do that."

My Faith Choice

This week I will bring the healing love of forgiveness to someone. I will

_____

_____.

An Act of Contrition

The word contrition means "sorrow." Learn this or another act of contrition by heart. Pray it daily.

**My God,
I am sorry for my sins with all my heart.
In choosing to do wrong
and failing to do good,
I have sinned against you
whom I should love above all things.
I firmly intend, with your help,
to do penance, to sin no more,
and to avoid whatever leads me to sin.
Our Savior Jesus Christ
suffered and died for us.
In his name, my God, have mercy.**

We Remember

Circle the T next to the true statements. Circle the F next to the false statements. Make each false statement true.

1. Sin hurts our friendship with God.   **T   F**

2. In the sacrament of Reconciliation we confess our sins to a priest.   **T   F**

3. We receive the sacrament of the Anointing of the Sick when we are healthy.   **T   F**

4. Jesus healed the sick during his life on earth.   **T   F**

To Help You Remember

1. In the sacrament of Reconciliation God always forgives us our sins when we are truly sorry.

2. In Reconciliation the Holy Spirit helps us to not sin again.

3. In the sacrament of the Anointing of the Sick, our faith and trust in God are made stronger.

This Week . . .

In chapter 15, "We Celebrate God's Healing Love," your child learned more about the forgiving and healing love of God. Through Christ we have been saved from sin and reconciled with God and with all creation. The sins we commit after Baptism are forgiven through the power of the Holy Spirit in the sacrament of Reconciliation. Christ's victory is also a victory over suffering and death. In the sacrament of the Anointing of the Sick, we receive the grace to join our sufferings to Christ's. Our faith and trust in God is strengthened.

For more on the teachings of the Catholic Church on the Sacraments of Healing, Reconciliation, and Anointing of the Sick, see *Catechism of the Catholic Church* paragraph numbers 1420–1484 and 1499–1525.

Sharing God's Word

Read together the parable of the Forgiving Father in Luke 15:11–24 or read the adaptation of the parable on page 130. Emphasize that the actions of the loving father in the parable tell us about God's love for us. God will always forgive us when we are sorry for our sins.

Praying

In this chapter your child prayed an act of contrition. Read and pray together the prayer on page 135.

Making a Difference

Choose one of the following activities to do as a family or design a similar activity of your own.

- Make a list of all the words you can use to ask for forgiveness or say to someone who asks for your forgiveness. Talk about how much better we feel after we ask to be forgiven or when someone forgives us.

- Recall that God always forgives us our sins when we are sorry. Invite family members to share their ideas on why forgiveness is an essential quality of the Christian family.

- Jesus often healed the sick during his life on earth. Talk about the ways your family cares for one another when someone in your family is sick.

For more ideas on ways your family can live your faith, visit the "Faith First for Families" page at **www.FaithFirst.com**. You are only a click away from "Family Prayer."

The Wedding Feast in Cana

A Scripture Story

16

THERE WAS A MARRIAGE IN CANA

We Pray

The LORD, our God,
  is near
  to all who call
  upon him.
  Based on Psalm 145:18

God the Father, Son, and Holy Spirit, strengthen the faith of our families and through them, bless the Church. Amen.

Why are weddings such happy times?

The Gospel of John tells us that Jesus went to a wedding celebration in the village of Cana.

What do you remember about what happened at the wedding?

Jesus changing water into wine at the marriage celebration in Cana

137

Bible Background

Faith Focus

What does the story of the wedding in Cana tell us about God?

Faith Words

miracle
A miracle is a sign of God's presence and power at work in our world.

Jewish Weddings in Jesus' Time

During Jesus' time many Jewish weddings took place in the fall of the year. The wedding began in the evening. The groom met the bride at her house. Then the wedding party walked from the bride's house to the groom's house for the ceremony.

The next day the bride and groom and everyone began celebrating the wedding. People danced and sang and opened presents. For seven days the bridegroom and his family provided food and wine for all the guests. The bridegroom kept the wine used at the wedding in large stone, or pottery, jars.

Why is the celebration of marriage a happy and joyous celebration?

Jesus Helps a Newly Married Couple

Once Jesus, his mother, and the disciples went to a wedding in Cana in Galilee. During the wedding, Mary saw that the groom's family had run out of wine. Act out what happens next.

Mary: Jesus, they have no wine left.

Jesus: How can I help them, Mother?

Mary: (*to the servants*) Do whatever he tells you.

Jesus: (*to the servants*) Fill the six stone jars with water.

Narrator: The servants filled the six jars with water from a well. Each jar held twenty to thirty gallons of water.

Jesus: Take some of what is in the jars and give it to the head servant.

Head servant: (*tastes wine and looks surprised*) People serve their best wine first. Then after people eat, they serve their cheaper wine. But you have kept the best wine to serve last.

Narrator: Jesus changed the water into wine. Many of his disciples came to believe in Jesus because of what he did.

Based on John 2:3–11

Pretend you are one of Jesus' disciples at the wedding. Share what you might say to Jesus when you hear what he did.

_____

_____

_____

_____

_____

_____

The Healing of the Blind Beggar
(Luke 18:35–43)

God Is with Us

Jesus performed a **miracle** when he changed the water into wine. A miracle is a sign of God's presence and power at work in our world. Through miracles God invites us to believe and trust in him. Seeing this miracle of water changed into wine, Jesus' followers began to believe that he was sent by God.

The New Testament tells us that Jesus worked many other miracles. People came to have faith and trust in God because of the miracles Jesus performed.

The pictures on this page show two other miracles of Jesus. In the box draw or write about another miracle story of Jesus that you know. Write the name of the story under the picture.

The Healing of a Paralyzed Man
(Luke 5:17–20)

Our Church Makes a Difference

Our Catholic Faith

Collection at Mass

All Catholics are called to serve other people as the people of Saint Mark's parish do. The money that is collected at Mass during the collection is used by a parish to serve people in many ways. One way the money is sometimes used is to help people who are out of work. Serving people in this and other ways is a sign of God's love for them.

Signs of God's Love

The Catholic community of Saint Mark the Evangelist is a sign that God is always at work in the world. Each month the people of the parish collect canned food, used clothing, furniture, and everyday items such as soap, shampoo, and school supplies.

One Sunday each month, they fill a truck with the things the people of Saint Mark's wish to share with people in need. They bring everything they have gathered that month to the people of a parish they have adopted.

When we do these things, we are signs of God's love for people. Through the things we do and say God invites people to believe and trust in him.

Describe some of the ways your parish is a sign of God's love for people. How can you join with them in doing these things?

What Difference Does Faith Make in My Life?

God is at work in the world. When you help others, you help people come to know God's love. God works through you to invite people to believe and trust in him.

Complete these sentences to show how you come to know God's love.

Signs of God

Each time I see a _____
I believe God is at work in the world.

Each time I hear a _____
I believe God is at work in the world.

Each time I _____
I am a sign of God at work in the world.

My Faith Choice

This week I will be a sign of God at work in the world. I will

_____

_____ .

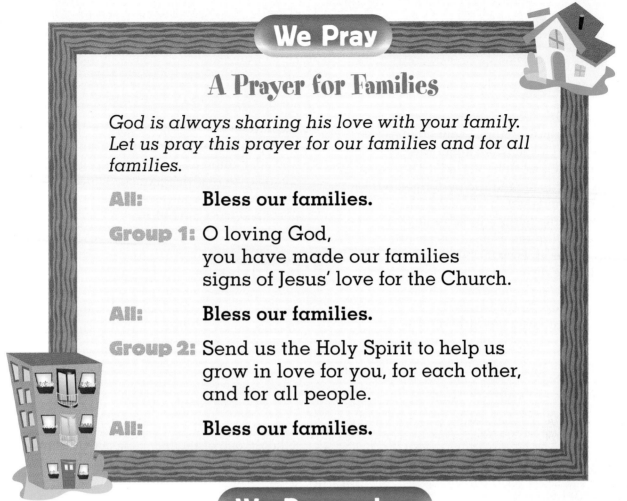

We Pray

A Prayer for Families

God is always sharing his love with your family. Let us pray this prayer for our families and for all families.

All: **Bless our families.**

Group 1: O loving God,
you have made our families
signs of Jesus' love for the Church.

All: **Bless our families.**

Group 2: Send us the Holy Spirit to help us
grow in love for you, for each other,
and for all people.

All: **Bless our families.**

We Remember

Unscramble the purple words. Write the words on the lines to complete the sentences.

1. Jesus and his mother went to a wedding in the town of **nCaa**.

   _____

2. At the wedding Jesus performed the **acmiler** of changing the water in six stone jars into wine.

   _____

3. When Jesus' disciples saw him change the water into wine, they came to **evebeli** he was sent to them by God.

   _____

To Help You Remember

1. Jesus performed a miracle at the wedding in Cana to show that God's power is at work in the world.

2. When Jesus changed water into wine, his disciples came to believe he was sent by God.

3. Jesus' miracle in Cana helped people trust in God.

This Week . . .

In chapter 16, "The Wedding Feast in Cana: A Scripture Story," your child learned the Gospel story about the wedding in Cana (John 2:1–11). The focus of this story is the miracle performed by Jesus of turning water into wine. The miracles in the Scriptures serve an important purpose. They are signs of God's power at work in the world. Miracles are divine invitations to believe and trust in God's goodness, which is always at work in the world. They are invitations to love God with our whole heart and to share that love with others.

For more on the teaching of the Catholic Church on miracles, see *Catechism of the Catholic Church* paragraph numbers 156, 515, 547–49, and 1335.

Sharing God's Word

Read together the Bible story in John 2:1–11 about the wedding in Cana or read the adaptation of the story on page 139. Emphasize that this miracle helped the disciples believe in Jesus and grow in their faith and trust in God.

Praying

In this chapter your child prayed a prayer for families. Read and pray together the prayer on page 143.

Making a Difference

Choose one of the following activities to do as a family or design a similar activity of your own.

- Jesus performed a miracle when he turned the water into wine. Read one or more of these miracle stories: Luke 18:35–43, Mark 4:35–41, or Luke 5:17–20. Share what each story helps you come to know about God.

- When we help people, we are signs of God's love. As a family, choose to do one thing this week to be a sign of God's love.

- At dinnertime this week think about and name the signs of God's love each family member has experienced that day. Include a prayer of thanksgiving as part of your mealtime prayer.

For more ideas on ways your family can live your faith, visit the "Faith First for Families" page at **www.FaithFirst.com**. Check out "Bible Stories." Read and discuss the Bible story together.

The Sacraments of Service

17

We Pray

LORD, help me
understand how
you want me to live.
Based on Psalm 119:34

**Father, send
the Holy Spirit
to help your
Church serve the
People of God.
Amen.**

*When have you done
something really
difficult to help
someone else?*

People do many
things each day to
help us. God calls
some members of the
Church to help and
serve all the People
of God.

*What two sacraments
dedicate people to
serve the whole
community of the
Church?*

We Are Called to Serve

Faith Focus

How do bishops, priests, deacons, and married people serve the people of the Church?

Faith Words

Holy Orders

Holy Orders is the sacrament in which a baptized man is ordained a bishop, priest, or deacon to serve the whole Church his whole life long.

Matrimony

Matrimony is the sacrament in which a baptized man and a baptized woman make lifelong promises to serve the Church as a married couple.

Jesus Teaches Us to Serve

Jesus served God and the People of God. God calls every baptized person to share in Jesus' life and work. At the Last Supper Jesus taught his Apostles to serve others as he did.

During the meal Jesus got up from the table. He poured water into a bowl and began to wash his disciples' feet. He dried their feet with a towel. When Jesus finished, he said, "I have given you an example. Do what I have done."

Based on John 13:4–5, 15

At Baptism we receive the vocation to share in Jesus' life and work. The word *vocation* means "a calling." We can live our vocation in many ways. You live that calling now. When you grow up, you will make a decision about how you will follow Christ as an adult.

Write how you are living your vocation as a follower of Christ now. Write how you might live it as an adult.

Holy Orders

God gives some members of the Church the vocation to be bishops, priests, or deacons. This vocation is celebrated in the sacrament of **Holy Orders.** Holy Orders is one of the two Sacraments at the Service of Communion. Like Baptism and Confirmation, Holy Orders cannot be repeated. It marks the man who receives this sacrament with a permanent, spiritual mark, or character.

Bishops, priests, and deacons are ordained to serve the whole Church. They have served the Church from the days of the Apostles. A baptized man is ordained forever. Only bishops can ordain other bishops, priests, and deacons.

Bishops lead the people in worshiping God. They teach people about the faith. They guide the Church to live as Jesus taught. Priests are coworkers with bishops in their work. Bishops and priests serve the Church in Jesus' name and live their life unmarried. Deacons are not priests. They help bishops and work with priests.

Name ways you have seen a bishop, priest, or deacon serve people.

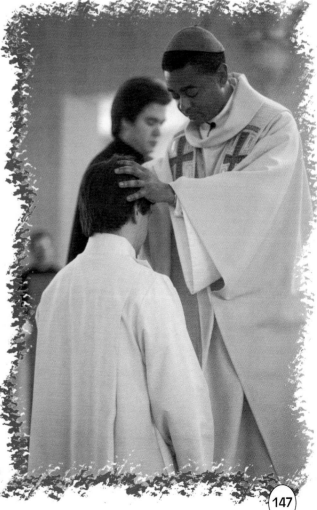

Faith-Filled People

Deacons

Deacons assist at worship. They proclaim and preach the word of God. They minister the sacrament of Baptism and can lead the sacrament of Matrimony. They visit and pray with people who are sick. They help people who are in need of clothing, food, or a home.

A bishop ordaining a priest

Matrimony

God calls some members of the Church to marry. A baptized man and a baptized woman celebrate marriage in the sacrament of **Matrimony.** They serve the Church as a married couple.

In Matrimony a man and a woman freely promise to always love and be faithful to each other. They accept the gift of children. They promise to treat each other with honor and respect.

The Holy Spirit helps husbands and wives love one another just as Jesus loves his Church. Parents and children work together to live the Gospel. Christian families have the vocation to be signs of God's love in the world.

Tell how the people in the pictures are being signs of God's love for one another. In the blank box draw or write about how your family is a sign of God's love.

Catholic Relief Services

The Church serves everyone. At Baptism we receive a lighted candle and promise to live as lights in the world. The Catholic bishops in the United States have organized the Catholic Relief Services to help Catholics in America keep that promise.

Catholic Relief Services brings together the people of the Catholic Church in the United States to help people. Through the Catholic Relief Services' Thanksgiving Clothing Appeal, Catholics in America have shared millions of pounds of clothing with people in need.

Catholic Relief Services workers go wherever help is needed. They serve people in need in countries all over the world.

Describe one way you might serve people in your community.

Our Catholic Faith

The Pope

The pope is the pastor of the whole Church. Helped by the Holy Spirit, the pope guides the whole Church in serving people all over the world. The pope is the bishop of Rome. He is the successor of Saint Peter the Apostle. Jesus chose Peter the Apostle to be the first pastor of the whole Church.

Children in Burundi, East Africa, receiving help from Catholic Relief Services

What Difference Does Faith Make in My Life?

You have been called by God to serve others as a follower of Jesus. The Holy Spirit helps you live that calling now in many ways.

The words in the border name some of the qualities of a follower of Jesus. Choose one of these qualities and color in the letters. Write or draw how you can serve others when you live that quality.

RESPECTFUL   GENEROUS

LOVING CARING

PATIENT KIND

Followers of Jesus

FORGIVING   HONEST

My Faith Choice

This week I will choose one of the words above and put it into practice to serve other people. I will

_____

_____.

Bless Your Servants

Pray this prayer of intercession. In a prayer of intercession we ask God to bless others.

Leader: Let us pray for all who serve the Church. For all priests, deacons, and bishops,

All: **we ask your blessing, Lord.**

Leader: For all our parents and others who teach us how to love you and others,

All: **we ask your blessing, Lord.**

Leader: For everyone who works to build up the Church,

All: **we ask your blessing, Lord.**

Leader: We make our prayer in the name of your Son, Jesus.

All: **Amen.**

We Remember

Complete each sentence. Use the words in the word bank.

Baptism   Holy Orders   Matrimony

1. In _____ a baptized man is ordained a bishop, priest, or deacon.

2. At _____ all Christians receive the vocation to share in Jesus' work.

3. In _____ a baptized man and a baptized woman promise to always love and be faithful to each other.

To Help You Remember

1. Bishops and priests lead people in worshiping God and learning and living their faith.

2. Deacons help bishops and work with priests.

3. A baptized man and a baptized woman who receive the sacrament of Matrimony are a sign of God's love in the world.

This Week . . .

In chapter 17, "The Sacraments of Service," your child learned that all the baptized have the vocation to serve God and other people as Jesus did. Some of the baptized are called to serve the whole Church. This call is celebrated in the two Sacraments at the Service of Communion, Holy Orders and Matrimony. Holy Orders is the sacrament through which a baptized man is ordained a bishop, a priest, or a deacon. Matrimony is the sacrament that unites a baptized man and a baptized woman forever in love as husband and wife.

For more on the teachings of the Catholic Church on the Sacraments at the Service of Communion, see *Catechism of the Catholic Church* paragraph numbers 1533–1589 and 1601–1658.

Sharing God's Word

Read together the Bible story in John 13:1–17 about Jesus washing the disciples' feet or read the adaptation of the story on page 146. Emphasize that at the Last Supper Jesus taught the disciples to serve others as he did.

Praying

In this chapter your child prayed a prayer of intercession asking God to bless all those who serve the Church. Read and pray together the prayer on page 151.

Making a Difference

Choose one of the following activities to do as a family or design a similar activity of your own.

- As a family, choose one thing you can do this week to serve others as Jesus did.

- Name some of the ways young people can keep the promises made at Baptism and live as signs of God's love in the world. Talk about how a family can help the young people in a family keep those promises.

- Talk about how your family can serve others and be a sign of God's love. Join with other members of your family and do one of those things.

For more ideas on ways your family can live your faith, visit the "Faith First for Families" page at **www.FaithFirst.com**. Visit the "Games" site this week. Ask your child to show you the game they like most. Play it together.

A. The Best Word or Phrase

Complete the sentences. Circle the best choice under each sentence.

1. The Church gathers all year long to _____ God.
   - a. worship
   - b. greet
   - c. sing to

2. The Church's year of worship is called the _____ .
   - a. holy year
   - b. Christian year
   - c. liturgical year

3. _____ includes all the weeks of the Church's year that are not part of Advent, Christmas, Lent, or Easter.
   - a. Springtime
   - b. Wintertime
   - c. Ordinary Time

4. _____ completes our Baptism and helps us bring Jesus to the world.
   - a. Confirmation
   - b. Penance
   - c. Marriage

5. The Church brings the _____ to the elderly, sick, or those in the hospital.
   - a. Bible
   - b. Blessed Sacrament
   - c. collection

6. Reconciliation is one of the two Sacraments of _____ .
   - a. Initiation
   - b. Healing
   - c. Service

7. A _____ is a sign of God's power at work in the world.
   - a. miracle
   - b. parable
   - c. Bible

8. Holy Orders and _____ are the two Sacraments at the Service of Communion.
   - a. Baptism
   - b. Confirmation
   - c. Matrimony

B. Words and Meanings

Draw a line to connect the words to their clues.

Words

Baptism

Confirmation

Eucharist

Reconciliation

Anointing of the Sick

Matrimony

Holy Orders

Clues

The grace of Baptism is strengthened.

Sins committed after Baptism are forgiven.

A person is born into the Church family.

Bread and wine become the Body and Blood of Christ.

A baptized man and a baptized woman become husband and wife.

A baptized man becomes a bishop, priest, or deacon.

We are strengthened in times of serious illness.

C. What I Have Learned

1. *What are two new things you learned in this unit?*

   _____

   _____

2. *Look back at the list of faith words on page 96. Circle the words you now know. Tell your group the meaning of two of the words.*

D. From a Scripture Story

Complete the diagram. Tell how the Pharisee and the tax collector in the parable are alike and how they are different.

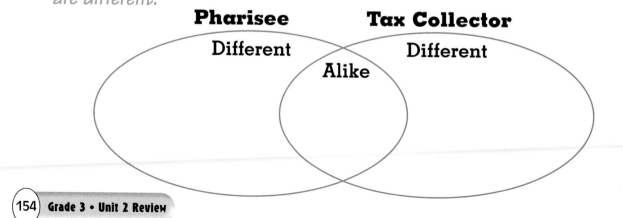

Pharisee   **Tax Collector**

Different   Different

Alike

Unit 3 • We Live

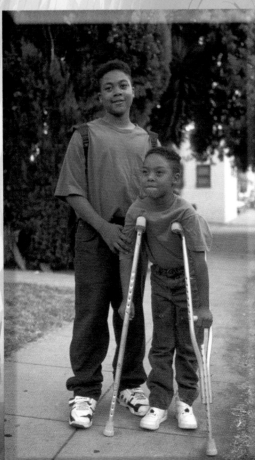

What things do Christians do to live the Commandments?

Getting Ready

What I Have Learned

What is something you already know about these faith words?

Loving God

_____

_____

Loving others

_____

_____

Words to Know

Put an X next to the faith words you know. Put a ? next to the faith words you need to know more about.

Faith Words

_____ Covenant

_____ Great Commandment

_____ Ten Commandments

_____ obey

_____ Psalms

_____ stewards

_____ grace

_____ heaven

Questions I Have

What question would you like to ask about living the Ten Commandments?

_____

_____

A Scripture Story

Jesus teaching the Great Commandment

How does the Great Commandment help us live as followers of Jesus?

Jesus Teaches Us How to Love

A Scripture Story

We Pray

Teach me your ways,
  O LORD.
        Based on Psalm 119:33

**God of love,
may we do what
you ask of us.**
        Amen.

*What promises have
you made?*

Promises are
important to keep.
The Bible tells us that
God made and keeps
his promises to us.

*What did God
promise us?*

Bible Background

How can we show that we are friends of God?

Covenant
The Covenant is the solemn agreement of friendship made between God and his people.

Great Commandment
The Great Commandment is the commandment of love that all of God's laws depend on.

God's Special Promise

In the very beginning of the Bible we read that our first parents made a promise to God. They promised to obey God. But our first parents, whom the Bible calls Adam and Eve, did not keep their promise and sinned. We call this broken promise original sin. They lost the happiness God had given them.

God made a promise to the first humans after they sinned. He would send someone to make people and God friends again. This promise is called the **Covenant.**

God kept his promise. He sent his Son, Jesus. Jesus made us friends with God again.

Put a ✔ next to the ways that show you are living as a friend of God. Then write two more ways you are living as a friend of God.

❑ Take part in Mass on Sunday.

❑ Honor my parents.

❑ Tell the truth.

❑ Play fairly at recess.

❑ Respect what belongs to others.

_____

_____

The Great Commandment

Jesus taught what it means to live the Covenant. He reminded God's people to live the **Great Commandment.** Read what happened.

A teacher of the law asked Jesus, "Which of the commandments of God is the greatest commandment?"

Jesus answered, "'Love God with all your heart, soul, and mind.' This is the greatest and the first commandment."

Jesus did not stop there. He continued, "The second commandment is like it: 'You shall love your neighbor as yourself.' The whole law depends on these two commandments."

Based on Matthew 22:35–40

These two commandments of God make up the Great Commandment. When we live the Great Commandment, we live the Covenant. We keep our promises to God.

Name two ways the Church helps us live the Great Commandment.

159

Love God and Others

We keep our promises to God when we live the Great Commandment. The Great Commandment has two parts. The first part is that we are to love God. The second part is that we are to love others as we love ourselves. The two parts form one Great Commandment.

We need to live both parts of the Great Commandment. We cannot only show our love for God through prayer and worship. We also need to show our love for God by the way we treat ourselves and other people.

Jesus taught us that loving others includes loving our enemies. This is not an easy thing to do.

Tell how the children in the pictures are living the Great Commandment. In the space write about or draw yourself living the Great Commandment.

Our Church Makes a Difference

Virtues

You teach others by how you act. One way you do this is by living the virtues. Virtues are habits of doing good things. Living a life of virtue means getting into the habit of doing good things for others and for yourself. It is what living the Great Commandment is all about.

Teaching Communities

There have been many great teachers in our Church. Some of these teachers formed religious communities that are dedicated to teaching young people. Saint Angela Merici and Saint John Baptist de La Salle are two of these teachers.

Saint Angela Merici founded the Company of St. Ursula. The Ursuline Sisters were the first religious community of women dedicated to teaching.

Saint John Baptist de La Salle founded the Brothers of the Christian Schools. The Christian Brothers are dedicated to teaching young people, especially the poor. In 1950, the Church proclaimed de La Salle the patron of all teachers.

In all their teaching, the Ursulines and the Christian Brothers teach young people to grow in their love for Jesus. Their schools teach young people to prepare for the coming of the kingdom of God by living the Great Commandment.

Name someone who teaches you how to live the Great Commandment.

What Difference Does Faith Make in My Life?

The Holy Spirit is always teaching you to live the Great Commandment.

Draw or write about yourself living the Great Commandment. Share your story with someone.

Living the Great Commandment

My Faith Choice

This week I will try to live the Great Commandment. I will

_____

_____.

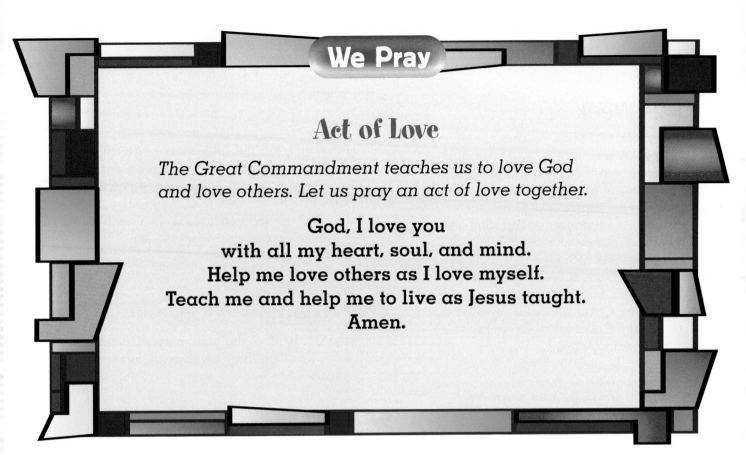

Act of Love

The Great Commandment teaches us to love God and love others. Let us pray an act of love together.

God, I love you
with all my heart, soul, and mind.
Help me love others as I love myself.
Teach me and help me to live as Jesus taught.
Amen.

We Remember

Circle the **T** *next to the statement if it is true. Circle the* **F** *if the statement is false. Make any false statements true.*

1. Original sin is the name we give to Adam and Eve breaking their promise to God.   **T   F**

2. The Commandment is the solemn agreement of friendship made between God and his people.   **T   F**

3. The Great Commandment shows us how to find true happiness with God now on earth and forever in heaven.   **T   F**

To Help You Remember

1. We show we are friends of God when we keep our promise to live the Covenant.

2. We live the Covenant when we love God with our whole heart.

3. We live the Covenant when we love other people as we love ourselves.

This Week . . .

In chapter 18, "Jesus Teaches Us How to Love: A Scripture Story," your child learned about the Covenant, or solemn agreement of friendship made between God and his people. The Covenant included the promise to send someone to restore all people to a life of friendship and happiness with God now and forever in heaven. God fulfilled this promise and sent his Son, Jesus, the new and everlasting Covenant. Jesus revealed that we live the Covenant when we live the Great Commandment.

For more on the teachings of the Catholic Church on the Covenant and the Great Commandment, see *Catechism of the Catholic Church* paragraph numbers 54–67, 2052–2055, and 2083.

Sharing God's Word

Read together the Bible story in Matthew 22:34–40 about the Great Commandment or read the adaptation of the story on page 159. Emphasize that Jesus taught that all of the Law of God depends on the Great Commandment.

Praying

In this chapter your child prayed an act of love. Read and pray together the prayer on page 163.

Making a Difference

Choose one of the following activities to do as a family or design a similar activity of your own.

- Invite each family member to share the names of people who have taught them to live the Great Commandment. Thank God for these wonderful people!

- Catechists, or religion teachers, live the Great Commandment when they teach us. Make thank-you cards for your catechists. Thank them for teaching you about the Great Commandment.

- Talk about how your family can live the Great Commandment. As a family, choose one thing you can do this week to live the Great Commandment.

For more ideas on ways your family can live your faith, visit the "Faith First for Families" page at **www.FaithFirst.com**. Click on "Make a Difference" for ideas on how your family can live the Great Commandment.

The Ten Commandments Teach Us to Love

We Pray

Blessed is the child of God who finds happiness in the law of the LORD.

Based on Psalm 1:1–2

Lord God, thank you for sending us Jesus to teach us how to live as your friends. **Amen.**

Why do you think it is important to have rules or laws?

Everywhere we go there are rules and laws we must obey. God gave us the Ten Commandments to teach us to love God, others, and ourselves.

What are some of the Ten Commandments you already know?

Tablets containing the Ten Commandments

 165

Living the Commandments

Faith Focus

How do the Ten Commandments help us to love God?

Faith Words

Ten Commandments
The Ten Commandments are the laws God gave to Moses on Mount Sinai. They guide us to love God and love others as we love ourselves.

God's Laws

The Bible tells many stories about the Covenant. We read about the covenants God made with Noah and with Abraham. Many years after Abraham, God made a covenant with Moses and God's people, the Israelites. God called Moses up to the top of Mount Sinai and gave him the **Ten Commandments.** Moses took the Commandments that God had given him and went down from the mountain. He explained the laws to the Israelites, who agreed to obey them. The Ten Commandments helped the Israelites to live as God's special people.

Read the Ten Commandments on page 287. Describe why living the Ten Commandments is important.

Showing Our Love for God

The first three Commandments help us show our love for God. The First Commandment teaches that we are to worship only God. We are to love and honor God above all else. The First Commandment is

"I am the LORD your God. You shall not have other gods before me."

Based on Exodus 20:2–3

The Second Commandment teaches that we are to respect the name of God. We are to use God's name truthfully. The Second Commandment is

"You shall not take the name of the LORD your God in vain." Exodus 20:7

The Third Commandment teaches that we are to keep Sunday holy. Sunday is the Lord's Day. Catholics must take part in the celebration of Mass on Saturday evening or Sunday. The Third Commandment is

"Remember to keep holy the LORD's Day." Based on Exodus 20:8

Name one way you can live each of the first three Commandments.

God Is Love

The Bible tells us that God is love. The three Persons in God the Holy Trinity love each other with a perfect love.

Jesus taught us that God loves us and shares his love with us. We share in the love of God the Father, God the Son, and God the Holy Spirit. We are to love God and one another as God loves us.

Unscramble the letters. Discover how we are to love others. Let the capital letters help you.

How to Love

evoL   sa

" _____ _____

oGd   sevol   oyu.

_____ _____ _____."

Based on Matthew 5:48

Churches

In the first two hundred years after the first Pentecost, there were no churches like the ones we have today. The community of the Church gathered in homes to hear the Scriptures read, to learn the teachings of the Apostles, and to celebrate Eucharist. It was only after the emperor of Rome gave Christians permission to worship in public that Christians began to build churches.

The first churches were called basilicas. The basilica of Saint John Lateran is the oldest basilica in Rome. It is the cathedral of the bishop of Rome, the pope.

There are many different types of churches. Every church is a sign of the faith in God of the people who built it.

Take a tour of your church. How is your church a sign of the faith of the people of your parish community?

Our Catholic Faith

Cathedrals

The cathedral is the main church of the archdiocese or diocese. It is the archbishop's or bishop's church. The word *cathedral* comes from the word *cathedra* which means "chair." The bishop's chair is a symbol that the bishop is the chief teacher and celebrant of the liturgy of the diocese in the cathedral.

St. Mary of the Lake, White Bear Lake, Minnesota

St. John Lateran, Rome, Italy

St. Mary's, Miami, Florida

What Difference Does Faith Make in My Life?

You and your family make Sunday a special day. You join other families in your parish for the celebration of Mass. You spend time together and show your love for God and for one another.

Work with two partners. Write out a role-play of a family deciding to make Sunday a day to celebrate their love for God and others. Act out your role-play for your class.

God's Special Day

_____

_____

_____

_____

_____

My Faith Choice

This week I will show God and others my love and respect for God. I will

_____

_____.

Prayer of Adoration

A prayer of adoration tells God that he alone is God. Pray this prayer together.

Leader: God, we cannot see you, yet we do believe.
All: **We adore you, O God.**
Leader: There is no other God but you.
All: **We adore you, O God.**
Leader: We know you are our God because your Son has told us so.
All: **We adore you, O God.**
Leader: We make our prayer in his name.
All: **Amen.**

We Remember

Complete the Commandments. Fill in the missing words.

1. I am the LORD your _____.
   You shall not have other gods before me.

2. You shall not take the _____
   of the LORD your _____ in vain.

3. Remember to keep _____
   the _____ Day.

To Help You Remember

1. The First Commandment teaches us to love God above all else.

2. The Second Commandment teaches us to love God by honoring his name.

3. The Third Commandment teaches us to love God by keeping the Lord's Day holy.

This Week . . .

In chapter 19, "The Ten Commandments Teach Us to Love," your child learned that God gave us the Ten Commandments. The Commandments teach us to love God, ourselves, and others. God gave the Commandments to Moses on Mount Sinai. The First, Second, and Third Commandments teach us to show our love and respect for God, who is love, above all else.

For more on the teachings of the Catholic Church on the Trinity as a divine communion of love and on the first three Commandments, see *Catechism of the Catholic Church* paragraph numbers 218–221, 253–256, 2084–2132 (First Commandment), 2142–2159 (Second Commandment), and 2168–2188 (Third Commandment).

Sharing God's Word

Read together the story in Exodus 20:2–17 about the Ten Commandments. Emphasize that the Ten Commandments teach us how to live the Great Commandment.

Praying

In this chapter your child prayed a prayer of adoration. Read and pray together the prayer on page 171.

Making a Difference

Choose one of the following activities to do as a family or design a similar activity of your own.

- Catholics genuflect to show their adoration and respect for God. Share and talk about other prayer gestures the members of your family use to show your love, adoration, and respect for God.

- Invite each family member to share the feast day or holy day of obligation that is their favorite. Talk about how each of these feasts or holy days helps your family show love and respect for God.

- Talk about the ways your family lives the Third Commandment and keeps the Lord's Day holy. As a family, choose one thing you can do this coming Sunday to make the Lord's Day special.

For more ideas on ways your family can live your faith, visit the "Faith First for Families" page at **www.FaithFirst.com**. This week pay special attention to "Questions Kids Ask."

We Love and Respect One Another

20

We Pray

LORD, help me
keep your
Commandments
with all my heart.
Based on Psalm 119:10

**Father, Son,
and Holy Spirit,
help us live
united in respect
and love.   Amen.**

*What would it be like
if everyone treated
one another with
respect?*

Each day we have
many opportunities
to treat one another
with respect. God
asks us to love and
respect one another.

*In what ways do the
Ten Commandments
teach us to show love
and respect for one
another?*

God Teaches Us the Way to Love

How do the last seven Commandments help us show our love for one another and for ourselves?

Faith Words

obey

To obey means to choose to follow the guidance of someone who is helping us live according to God's laws.

covet

To covet means to wrongfully want something that belongs to someone else.

The Fourth Commandment

The last seven of the Commandments teach about living the second part of the Great Commandment. They name the ways God wants us to love and respect others and ourselves.

The Fourth Commandment teaches that we honor our parents. We honor our parents when we listen carefully to what they say and we **obey** them.

We honor our parents when we show them how much we appreciate what they do for us. We do this when we care for our clothes, our books, our food, our homes, and all the things they provide for us. The Fourth Commandment is

"Honor your father and your mother."

Exodus 20:12

Discuss some of the ways family members honor and respect one another.

The Fifth and Sixth Commandments

The Fifth Commandment teaches that all life is sacred and belongs to God. We are to treat our bodies and the bodies of others with respect and care. We are to avoid doing things that we know are dangerous and can harm us. The Fifth Commandment is

"You shall not kill." Exodus 20:13

The Sixth Commandment teaches that married people are to be faithful in their relationship. A husband and wife are always to love and honor each other. We live this Commandment when we respect our bodies and those of others. The Sixth Commandment is

"You shall not commit adultery." Exodus 20:14

Choose one of the Commandments on these two pages and rewrite it in your own words.

What the Commandments Mean to Me

_____

_____

_____

_____

_____

_____

The Seventh Through Tenth Commandments

The Seventh Commandment teaches that we respect what belongs to other people. We are to treat people fairly and justly. We use the things that we borrow properly and return them when we are finished. The Seventh Commandment is

"You shall not steal." Exodus 20:15

The Eighth Commandment teaches that we are to be honest and truthful. We are not to tell lies. We are not to hurt people by the things we say about them. The Eighth Commandment is

"You shall not bear false witness against your neighbor." Exodus 20:16

The Ninth Commandment teaches us to respect the marriage of a man and a woman. We are to help families grow in love. The Ninth Commandment is

"You shall not covet your neighbor's wife." Exodus 20:17

The Tenth Commandment teaches us not to be greedy or jealous. We are to share our things with people, especially with people in need. The Tenth Commandment is

"You shall not covet your neighbor's goods." Exodus 20:18

How are the actions of the children in the photos against the teachings of the Commandments? In the empty box, draw or write about children who are keeping the Tenth Commandment.

Our Parish Family

We treat others with love because of who we are! We are images of God. What does that mean? It means that when people look at us, they should come to know and love God by the things we say and do.

Our parish family is a sign of God's love for the people who live in our community. People feel welcome to stop and pray in our parish church. They see us working very hard at getting along. They see us sharing food with those who are hungry and clothes with those who need them. They see us visiting and caring for people who are sick.

When our parish family does these and other kind and loving things, we are living the Commandments. We are living as Jesus taught. We are signs of God's love.

✝ Our Catholic Faith

The Christian Family

The Christian family is like a church. It is a small community of the People of God. That is why the Church says that the Christian family is a domestic church. The word *domestic* means "belonging to the home." Being a good Christian begins at home with our families.

Describe things your parish family does that show it is an image of God.

177

What Difference Does Faith Make in My Life?

Each day you are kind and generous. You are trustworthy and honest. You respect your family and your friends. You are living the Ten Commandments as a child of God.

In the box explain how living the Commandments can make your community a better place.

My Faith Choice

This week I will try to make good decisions to respect myself and others. I will

_____

_____.

We Pray

We Pray for Others

We show our love for people by praying for them. Pray this prayer together.

Leader: God loves and cares for everyone. Let us ask God to hear our prayers.

For . . . *(add the name, or names, of people)*

All: **God of love, hear our prayer.**

Leader: God of love, hear the prayers of your children. Send the Holy Spirit to teach us ways to help those we pray for. We ask this through Christ our Lord.

All: **Amen.**

We Remember

Read this list of ways we can show our love and respect for ourselves and others. Write the number of the Commandment being followed in each one.

_____ We treat people fairly.

_____ We listen carefully to our parents and obey them.

_____ We tell the truth about others.

_____ We avoid things that are dangerous and can harm us.

To Help You Remember

1. The last seven of the Ten Commandments teach us how to live the second part of the Great Commandment.

2. They teach us to honor and respect people and the things that belong to them.

3. They teach us to be honest and truthful, kind and generous.

This Week . . .

In chapter 20, "We Love and Respect One Another," your child learned that the last seven of the Ten Commandments teach us to live the second part of the Great Commandment. These Commandments teach us to treat all people and ourselves as images of God and children of God. They teach us to respect and honor ourselves and others. They teach us to be honest and truthful, kind and generous.

For more on the teachings of the Catholic Church on the Ten Commandments, see *Catechism of the Catholic Church* paragraph numbers 2196, 2217–2246 (Fourth Commandment), 2258–2317 (Fifth Commandment), 2331–2391 (Sixth Commandment), 2401–2449 (Seventh Commandment), 2464–2503 (Eighth Commandment), 2514–2527 (Ninth Commandment), 2534–2550 (Tenth Commandment).

Sharing God's Word

Read together 1 John 4:11 about God's love. Emphasize that God commands us to love and respect others and ourselves.

Praying

In this chapter your child showed his or her love for people by praying for them. Read and pray together the prayer on page 179.

Making a Difference

Choose one of the following activities to do as a family or design a similar activity of your own.

- To obey means to follow the guidance of someone who is helping us live according to the Law of God. Invite each family member to share the names of people who help them live the Ten Commandments.

- The Fifth Commandment teaches us not to kill. Talk about the ways your family lives the Fifth Commandment. Then rewrite the Fifth Commandment in your own words.

- Look through your parish bulletin or visit your parish web site and name the ways your parish shows its love and respect for people.

For more ideas on ways your family can live your faith, visit the "Faith First for Families" page at **www.FaithFirst.com**. Click on "Contemporary Issues" for some interesting insights into living the Commandments.

21

The Psalms and Stewardship

A Scripture Story

We Pray

O God, the earth gives
us food.
You have blessed us.
Based on Psalm 67:6

**God the Creator,
we give you glory
for all the good
things we receive
from you. Amen.**

*Why do people enjoy
singing?*

People sing about
many things and
for many reasons.
One way we can
pray is by singing.
The Psalms are
prayer songs in the
Bible.

*What do you know
about the Psalms?*

Bible Background

Faith Focus

How do the Psalms help us pray and live as children of God the Creator?

Faith Words

Psalms

The Psalms are prayer songs found in the Bible in the Book of Psalms in the Old Testament.

stewards

Stewards are people who have the responsibility to care for things and to use them well.

Sacred Songs and Prayers

Long ago the Jewish people wrote sacred songs called psalms. The Jewish people prayed these songs. Jesus learned the **Psalms** and prayed them all his life. The first Christians prayed the Psalms. Today Christians still pray the Psalms every day.

Some psalms praise God and tell him about our needs. We call these laments. Other psalms give practical advice about how we can live as God's children. We call these wisdom psalms. We also pray the Psalms to thank God for the gifts of creation.

Use the code to discover one verse from a psalm of thanksgiving.

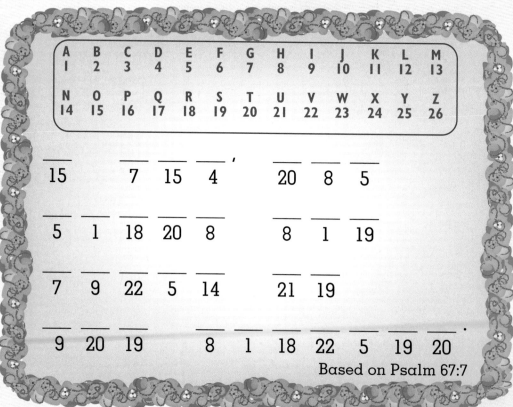

A	B	C	D	E	F	G	H	I	J	K	L	M
1	2	3	4	5	6	7	8	9	10	11	12	13

N	O	P	Q	R	S	T	U	V	W	X	Y	Z
14	15	16	17	18	19	20	21	22	23	24	25	26

15 __ 7 15 4 ' __ 20 8 5

5 1 18 20 8 __ 8 1 19

7 9 22 5 14 __ 21 19

9 20 19 __ 8 1 18 22 5 19 20 .

Based on Psalm 67:7

Psalm 104

Here is part of Psalm 104. We pray it to praise God and thank him for creation. It reminds us that God cares for all creation.

O God, you are great!

You make small streams become
    mighty rivers.
They flow through the tall
    mountains.
They give drink to all animals.
Birds rest and sing beside your
    waters.

LORD, we cannot count all the good
    things you have created.
    The earth is full of your creatures.

May your glory shine forever;
    may you be happy with everything
    you have made.
I will sing to God all my life.

Based on Psalm 104:1, 10–12, 24, 31, 33

Take a moment. Pray quietly in your heart the last seven lines from Psalm 104.

Caring for God's World

All creation gives glory to God. We give glory to God both when we pray and when we take care of creation.

The Bible tells us that God gave us the responsibility to care for creation. When we care for God's creation and use it well, we are good **stewards** of creation.

Good stewards live the Seventh Commandment. They take care of creation so that all people can enjoy and share it. They do not waste or misuse the gifts of creation. They share the beauty and goodness of creation with everyone.

Complete this prayer of thanksgiving. Share your prayer with your family.

Thanking God for Creation

O God, you are great and wonderful!
I thank you

for puppies and p_____ ,

for antelope and a _____ ,

for iguanas and i _____ ,

for elephants and e _____ .

Amen.

Christian Farmers

God gave farmers the fruits of the trees. God gave them the golden grain of the fields. God sent them the gentle rain and the warm sunrays. Farmers use these gifts to grow food to feed people.

At the Mass after the Harvest, Catholic farmers pray a psalm of thanksgiving. They pray verses from Psalm 67. They thank God for helping them be good stewards. The words they keep repeating are:

> O God, the earth has given us
>   its harvest.
> You have blessed us.
>
> Based on Psalm 67:7

God blesses the world by giving some Christians the vocation to be farmers. The Church and the whole world thank God for farmers. Farmers show us what it means to be good stewards of God's world.

Name some of the ways the members of your family are good stewards.

Our Catholic Faith

Mealtime Prayers

At mealtimes we thank God for the gift of creation. We say grace before and after we eat. We thank God for his blessings. We promise to share our blessings with people in need. We promise to be good stewards of God's creation.

What Difference Does Faith Make in My Life?

The Holy Spirit helps you live as a good steward of creation. When you are a good steward, your life is like a psalm. It is a prayer that gives glory to God.

Decorate this poster with symbols of creation and your favorite words from Psalm 104.

My Faith Choice

This week I will be a good steward of God's creation. I will

_____

_____.

Praise God

As you pray these verses from Psalm 150, pantomime the musical instruments named in the Psalm.

All: **Let all things praise God!**
Group 1: Praise God with blasts upon the horn.

All: **Let all things praise God!**
Group 2: Praise God with tambourines and flutes.

All: **Let all things praise God!**
Group 3: Praise God with sounding cymbals.

All: **Let all things praise God!**

Based on Psalm 150:3–6

We Remember

Write two ways you can be a good steward of God's creation.

To Help You Remember

1. Psalms help us pray many kinds of prayers.

2. Psalm 104 praises and thanks God for creation.

3. When we are good stewards of God's creation, we give praise and thanks to God.

 # With My Family

This Week . . .

In chapter 21, "The Psalms and Stewardship: A Scripture Story," your child learned about the Psalms. There are 150 psalms in the Book of Psalms in the Old Testament. Praying the Psalms was part of the prayer life of Jesus and the first Christians. Christians today pray the Psalms every day. There are many types of psalms. Each type of psalm helps us share our thoughts and feelings with God. Psalm 150 is a psalm giving praise and thanksgiving to God for the wonderful gift of creation. We become living psalms of praise when we are good stewards of God's creation.

For more on the teachings of the Catholic Church on the role of the Psalms in the prayer life of the Church, see *Catechism of the Catholic Church* paragraph numbers 716, 1176–1177, and 2585–2589.

Sharing God's Word

Read together Psalm 104. You can find Psalm 104 in the Bible or an adaptation of several verses of Psalm 104 on page 183. Emphasize that this psalm praises God and thanks God for creation.

Praying

In this chapter your child prayed Psalm 105:3–6. Read and pray together the prayer on page 187.

Making a Difference

Choose one of the following activities to do as a family or design a similar activity of your own.

- Design and make a poster that encourages people to be good stewards of God's creation. Try to come up with some creative slogans for your poster.

- Talk about how your family lives as good stewards of God's creation. As a family, choose to do one thing this week to be good stewards.

- Write a family prayer of thanksgiving. Thank God for all the wonderful gifts of creation. Use your prayer for family prayer this week.

For more ideas on ways your family can live your faith, visit the "Faith First for Families" page at **www.FaithFirst.com**. Click on the "Gospel Reflections" page this week and share some of the ideas together.

God Shares His Life with Us

22

We Pray

I believe I shall
  enjoy the LORD's
  goodness
in the land of the
  living.   Psalm 27:13

**O Lord our God,
may all live and
be happy with
you forever in
heaven.   Amen.**

*Who shares their life
with you?*

Our parents share
their love and lives
with us. God has
made us sharers in
his own life now and
in heaven.

*When you hear the
word heaven, what
do you think of?*

The Gift of Grace

Faith Focus

How does God make us sharers in his life and love?

Faith Words

grace
God's grace is the gift of God making us sharers in the life of the Holy Trinity. It is also the help God gives us to live a holy life.

heaven
Heaven is eternal life, or living forever in happiness with God after we die.

A Gift from God

God created us to share in the life and love of the Holy Trinity. Sharing in the life of God is a gift from God. We call this gift **grace.** The word *grace* means "gift" or "favor."

Sanctifying grace and actual grace are two kinds of grace. The word *sanctify* means "to make holy or sacred." Sanctifying grace is the grace we first receive at Baptism. It heals our soul of all sin and makes us holy. It makes us sharers in the very life of God.

Actual grace is the grace given to us by the Holy Spirit to help us make choices to live a holy life. Actual grace helps us overcome temptation. Temptation is everything that tries to lead us away from living as children of God. Actual grace helps us live as God wants us to live.

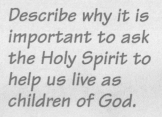

Describe why it is important to ask the Holy Spirit to help us live as children of God.

Jesus Promises Us Eternal Life

You have learned that Jesus was raised from the dead and ascended, or returned, to heaven. He now lives with God the Father and the Holy Spirit. God wants you to be happy with him forever too.

When your body dies, your soul still lives. You will live in a different way. God created you to live forever.

At the Last Supper Jesus promised his disciples,

"I am going to prepare a place for you so that we can be together."
Based on John 14:2–3

We call this promise the promise of eternal life. The word *eternal* means "forever." We call our eternal life of happiness with God **heaven.**

Find and circle the words in the puzzle that describe heaven.

Faith-Filled People

Patron Saints

The Church names some saints as patron saints. Patron saints are saints in heaven who have been chosen to pray in a special way for a person, a country, a town, a local parish church, or a group of people. Patron saints pray that we join them in heaven.

HAPPY

PEACEFUL

JOYFUL

D X D M S J T V

H O L P T O W Y

A B C D F Y M N

P E A C E F U L

P B L C O U G G

Y L N O P L Q T

Some Choose to Turn Away

Some people look for happiness that does not include God. Jesus told a story about people who do this. Jesus said,

"A man had a banquet. The guests he invited chose not to come. The man then said to his servants, 'Go into the streets and invite everyone you meet.' Soon the banquet hall was filled with guests."

Based on Luke 14:16, 18–21, 23

What are some things people can do to show they want to live in happiness with God?

The important point of the story is that God invites everyone to be happy with him forever in heaven. But some people choose not to accept God's invitation. Living separated from God forever after we die is called hell.

The Funeral Mass

The Church celebrates when a Catholic dies. We celebrate the Funeral Mass. We share the gifts of comfort and hope with the family, friends, and neighbors of the person who has died.

We see many signs that we believe in the gift of eternal life. We see a large white cloth, or pall. This reminds us of Baptism and that we share in God's life. We see the lighted Easter candle. This reminds us that Jesus was raised from the dead and we will live with him forever in heaven.

Describe how our belief in God's promise of heaven can help us when someone we love dies.

Our Catholic Faith

Incense

The Church uses incense at the conclusion of the Funeral Mass. Incense is one of the Church's sacramentals. When it is burned, incense produces smoke and a sweet aroma. The smoke rises quickly as a sign of our prayers going to heaven. This is a sign that we believe God listens to our prayers.

Final prayers at the conclusion of the funeral liturgy, using holy water and incense

Getting Ready

What I Have Learned

What is something you already know about these two faith terms?

Personal prayer

_____

_____

Public prayer

_____

_____

Words to Know

Put an X next to the faith words you know. Put a ? next to the faith words you need to know more about.

Faith Words

_____ prayer

_____ Abba

_____ petition

_____ intercession

_____ creed

_____ Hail Mary

Questions I Have

What questions would you like to ask about praying?

_____

_____

A Scripture Story

Mary visiting Elizabeth

Why did Mary visit Elizabeth?

Jesus Teaches Us to Pray

23

We Pray

Hear my words,
    O LORD.
To you I pray.

Psalm 5:2, 3

Our Father, who art in heaven, hallowed be thy name.   Amen.

Why is it important to spend time talking with those we care about?

God wants us to spend time talking with him.

When are some of the times you spend time with God?

Trusting God

Faith Focus

What are some ways Jesus teaches us to pray?

Faith Words

personal prayer
Personal prayer is spending time alone with God.

public prayer
Public prayer is praying with other people.

The Prayer of Jesus

When Jesus was on earth, he often spent time with God his Father in prayer. He prayed when he began his work on earth. He prayed when he chose his disciples. On the night before he died, Jesus prayed with his disciples at the Last Supper.

When Jesus was dying on the cross, he prayed,

"Father, forgive them. They do not know what they are doing." Just before he died, Jesus said, "Father, I give myself to you."

Based on Luke 23:34, 46

All Jesus' prayers show how much he trusts his Father. Trust is believing that a person loves us and will always be good and kind to us.

Jesus showed he trusted God the Father. Name some of the ways that you show your trust in God.

_____

_____

_____

_____

_____

Jesus Teaches Us the Our Father

When Jesus prayed to his Father, he sometimes used the word *Abba*. *Abba* is a word meaning "daddy" in the language Jesus spoke. It is a word that showed how much children trusted a parent. It showed they knew that the parent loved them.

One day Jesus' disciples were with him when he was praying. When he was finished, they asked Jesus to teach them to pray. Jesus said, "When you pray, say, 'Our Father'" (based on Matthew 6:9).

We call the prayer that Jesus taught the disciples the Lord's Prayer, or the Our Father. In this prayer we call God "Abba," our own Father.

The Church prays the Our Father every day. Name the times when you pray the Our Father.

Praying Alone and with Others

Jesus often left his disciples and went off to be alone with his Father. We, like Jesus, pray this way too. We enjoy being alone with God in prayer. We call this **personal prayer.**

Jesus also prayed with other people. Jesus prayed with people in Nazareth. He prayed with people in the Temple in Jerusalem. Praying with others is called **public prayer.** We pray this way too. We pray with our family at home. We pray with our Church community at Mass and at other times.

Draw a picture or write about yourself praying.

A People of Prayer

The Catholic Church uses many objects that help us pray. The crucifix reminds us that Jesus died for us and loves us. Lighted candles remind us that Jesus was raised from the dead. Statues of Joseph, of Mary, and of the other saints remind us that we belong to a community of people on earth and in heaven.

All these things are sacramentals. They help us raise our minds and hearts to God in prayer.

Name and describe the things that help you pray.

Our Catholic Faith

Churches

Churches are sometimes called "houses of prayer." They are also called "houses of God." We gather in our church to pray together and to pray alone. Our parish church reminds us that the followers of Jesus are a people of prayer.

What Difference Does Faith Make in My Life?

The Holy Spirit teaches you to pray. Every time you pray you show that you trust in God and God's love for you.

Put a ✔ next to the ways you now pray. Put a ★ next to the ways you would like to try to pray.

When, Where, How

___ 1. In my home

___ 2. At my parish church

___ 3. With my friends

___ 4. Kneeling down

___ 5. With my arms extended

___ 6. Every day

My Faith Choice

This week I will listen to the Holy Spirit and pray every day. I will

_____

_____.

Our Father

The Our Father is the prayer of all Christians.
The words of the Our Father teach us how to pray.

Leader: Let us raise our hands and pray as Jesus taught us.

All: Our Father, who art in heaven,
hallowed be thy name;
thy kingdom come;
thy will be done on earth as it is in heaven.
Give us this day our daily bread;
and forgive us our trespasses
as we forgive those who trespass against us;
and lead us not into temptation,
but deliver us from evil. Amen.

We Remember

Match the words in Column A with the words in Column B.

Column A	Column B
_____ 1. Abba	a. Prayer Jesus gave us
_____ 2. Our Father	b. Praying alone
_____ 3. private prayer	c. Praying with others
_____ 4. public prayer	d. A word that means "Father"

To Help You Remember

1. Jesus taught us to talk and listen to God the Father.

2. Jesus taught us to pray with trust.

3. Like Jesus, we pray alone with God and we pray together with other people.

This Week . . .

In chapter 23, "Jesus Teaches Us to Pray," your child learned about the prayer of Jesus and that Jesus taught us to pray. With trust, Jesus shared his thoughts and feelings with his Father. Jesus prayed for himself and for others. When his disciples asked Jesus to teach them to pray, he taught them to pray, "Our Father. . ." When we pray to God our Father, we pray with childlike trust and address God as Abba. We pray as children reaching out to parents who they know love them with a love that knows no limits.

For more on the teachings of the Catholic Church on prayer, see *Catechism of the Catholic Church* paragraph numbers 2558–2567, 2598–2619, 2700–2719.

Sharing God's Word

Read together the Bible story in Matthew 6:9–13 about Jesus teaching the disciples the Our Father. Emphasize that Jesus' prayers show how much he trusts his Father.

Praying

In this chapter your child prayed the Our Father. Read and pray together the Our Father on page 207.

Making a Difference

Choose one of the following activities to do as a family or design a similar activity of your own.

- When Jesus prayed, he placed his trust in God the Father. Invite family members to talk about how they show their trust in God.

- When you take part in Mass this week, spend time in the church after Mass. Look at the statues and all the other sacramentals that help you pray. Talk about how these things help you remember that God is always with you.

- Talk about the ways the members of your family pray alone and the ways you pray together. As a family, take time to pray each day this week.

For more ideas on ways your family can live your faith, visit the "Faith First for Families" page at **www.FaithFirst.com**. Click on "Family Prayer" to find a special prayer to pray together this week.

The Church Is a People of Prayer

24

We Pray

LORD our God, it is good to praise you.
Based on Psalm 92:2

Holy, holy, holy Lord, God of power and might. Heaven and earth are full of your glory.

What do you talk about with your family and friends?

People talk about many things with one another. We can talk to God about these and many other things.

What do you share with God when you pray?

Faith Focus

What are some of the ways we pray?

Faith Words

prayers of petition
Prayers of petition are prayers in which we ask God to help us.

prayers of intercession
Prayers of intercession are prayers in which we ask God to help others.

We Pray for Ourselves and for Other People

Jesus prayed in many ways. He prayed for himself and for other people. Like Jesus, we ask God to bless and help us. We ask God for forgiveness. We ask God to teach us how to live the Great Commandment. We pray that we will live in happiness with God and all the saints in heaven. We call these prayers for ourselves **prayers of petition.**

At other times we pray for other people. We pray for our family and friends. We pray for all people. We call these prayers for other people **prayers of intercession.**

When we pray for ourselves and for other people, we trust God listens to our prayers.

Look at the pictures on this page. With a partner talk about what the people in the pictures might be saying to God.

Faith-Filled People

Damien of Molokai

Blessed Damien of Molokai helped people who had a serious skin disease called leprosy. Nobody wanted to be near these people. Father Damien lived with them in their village so he could take care of them. We bless God for the gift of Blessed Damien of Molokai.

We Bless God

The bread and the wine we use at Mass are God's gifts to us. They are also our gifts to God. At Mass the priest takes the plate holding the bread that we have just brought to the altar. Lifting it up he prays a prayer of blessing. He prays,

Blessed are you, Lord, God of all creation. Through your goodness we have this bread to offer, which earth has given and human hands have made. It will become for us the bread of life.

We respond, "Blessed be God for ever."

The priest then holds up the cup of wine and prays another prayer of blessing. In a prayer of blessing, we tell God we know that everything good we have is God's gift to us. God blesses us, and we bless God.

Finish this prayer of blessing.

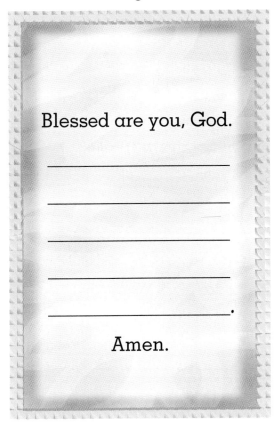

Blessed are you, God.

_____

_____

_____

_____

_____.

Amen.

We Praise God

There is only one God who is Father, Son, and Holy Spirit. We pray a prayer of praise when we tell God that only he is God. We love him above all else.

We Thank God

One day ten people who had a serious skin disease called leprosy came to Jesus. They asked Jesus to cure them of their sickness. Jesus cured all ten people. Here is what happened.

Only one of the ten thanked Jesus. He said, "Glory to God! I am healed!" Based on Luke 17:15–16

Invite all creation to praise God. Add to this prayer of praise.

God has done many wonderful things. It is important to say thank you to God for his blessings. When we do this, we are praying a prayer of thanksgiving.

Praise God

Praise God, sun and moon!

Praise God, _____.

Praise God, _____.

Praise God, _____.

Prayer Groups

When we come together to pray, Jesus tells us he is there with us. He said, "When you gather as my disciples, I am there with you" (based on Matthew 18:20). Prayer groups help us remember that Jesus is always with us when we pray together. Jesus is part of everything we do in his name. When we remember this, it makes a difference. Our whole life becomes a prayer.

Many parishes have prayer groups. Parishioners gather at the parish church or in homes to read the Scriptures and to pray together. They ask God's help for themselves and others. They bless God and ask God's blessing. Together they pray prayers of praise and thanks.

Describe some of the ways the people of your parish come together to pray.

Our Catholic Faith

Liturgy of the Hours

The Church gathers many times each day to pray. The Church celebrates the Eucharist and prays the Liturgy of the Hours. The Liturgy of the Hours is the official daily prayer of the Church.

What Difference Does Faith Make in My Life?

When you pray prayers of petition, intercession, blessing, praise, and thanksgiving, it is the Holy Spirit who is helping you pray.

Decorate this prayer poster.

Lord, hear my prayer.

My Faith Choice

This week I will pray every day. I will say a prayer of thanksgiving for

_____

_____

Blessed be God

The Divine Praises *is a prayer the Church gives us. Pray this part of the Divine Praises.*

Leader: Let us praise God. Let us join together and tell God he is wonderful and great. Blessed be God.

All: **Blessed be his holy name.**

Leader: Blessed be Jesus Christ, true God and true man.

All: **Blessed be the name of Jesus.**

Leader: Blessed be the Holy Spirit the Paraclete.

All: **Blessed be God in his angels and in his saints.**

We Remember

Find and circle the prayer words hidden in the puzzle. Use the words to tell a partner about prayer.

blessing   intercession   thanks
petition   praise

Q	W	W	B	P	E	T	I	T	I	O	N
L	K	Z	L	P	C	Z	O	I	U	Y	T
I	N	T	E	R	C	E	S	S	I	O	N
W	E	H	S	A	P	S	Q	W	E	R	T
R	W	A	S	I	O	S	A	D	F	G	H
T	Q	N	I	S	I	I	Z	X	C	V	B
Y	P	K	N	E	U	R	J	H	G	F	D
U	O	S	G	M	Y	G	U	Y	T	R	E

To Help You Remember

1. We pray for ourselves and for other people.

2. We bless God who gives us all our blessings.

3. We thank and praise God for all our blessings.

This Week . . .

In chapter 24, "The Church Is a People of Prayer," your child learned that the Church is a people of prayer. Prayer is at the heart of living and growing in our relationship with God. When we read the Bible and look at the life of Jesus, we discover five basic ways that the People of God express their prayers. We pray prayers of blessing and adoration, of petition, of intercession, of thanksgiving, and of praise. We pray to acknowledge and thank God the Creator and Savior and Sanctifier. We pray for ourselves and for others.

For more on the teachings of the Catholic Church on prayer, see *Catechism of the Catholic Church* paragraph numbers 2598–2691.

Sharing God's Word

Read together the Bible story in Matthew 18:20 about Jesus telling his disciples he is always with them when they gather in his name. Emphasize that Christians make their prayer in the name of Jesus.

Praying

In this chapter your child prayed a prayer of blessing God. Read and pray together the prayer on page 215.

Making a Difference

Choose one of the following activities to do as a family or design a similar activity of your own.

- When we pray for ourselves, we pray prayers of petition. When we pray for others, we pray prayers of intercession. As a family, take turns offering prayers of petition and intercession.

- When you take part in Mass this week, pay close attention to the prayer of the faithful. At dinnertime this week include a prayer of the faithful in your mealtime prayers.

- Find out if your parish has a prayer group who prays each day for the needs of your parish community. Contact the person in charge of the group. Have them include your family as a member of the group.

For more ideas on ways your family can live your faith, visit the "Faith First for Families" page at **www.FaithFirst.com**. Read this week's "Bible Story." Talk about the Bible story with your child.

We Profess Our Faith

25

We Pray

They believed God's word and sang his praise.
Based on Psalm 106:12

I believe in God the Father, God the Son, and God the Holy Spirit. Amen.

What are some of the things that you believe?

The creeds of the Church are summaries of what the Church believes. Each week we pray the creed at Mass.

What are two creeds the Church prays?

Priests in procession during the celebration of Easter Mass by the pope at St. Peter's Basilica in Rome

We Give Our Hearts to God

Faith Focus

Why do we pray with creeds?

Faith Words

creeds
Creeds are statements of what a person or a group believes.

Apostles' Creed
The Apostles' Creed is a brief summary of what the Church has believed from the time of the Apostles.

The Holy Spirit Helps Us Pray

Learning to pray is one of the most important things we do as Catholics. Saint Paul the Apostle said,

"We do not know how to pray as we ought." Romans 8:26

The Holy Spirit who is in our hearts helps and teaches us to pray. Every moment of every day, the Holy Spirit helps us give our hearts to God. The Holy Spirit is always praying in us and through us.

Fill in the chart by naming something you can pray about at different times during the day.

Praying During the Day

Morning   _____

Noon   _____

Afternoon   _____

Evening   _____

Bedtime   _____

We Pray the Creed at Mass

Saint Paul the Apostle told us, "No one can believe and say Jesus is God without the help of the Holy Spirit" (based on 1 Corinthians 12:3). The Church says what we believe in the **creeds** of the Church. When we pray the creeds of the Church, we profess our faith.

At Mass on Sundays, we make a profession of faith. We stand and pray the creed. The creed we usually pray is called the Nicene Creed.

Look up the Nicene Creed on page 284. Talk about what the Nicene Creed tells about what the Church believes.

"We believe in one God . . ."

Praying the Nicene Creed at Mass

The Apostles' Creed

The **Apostles' Creed** and the Nicene Creed are the two main creeds of the Church. The Apostles' Creed is a brief summary of what the Church has believed from the time of the Apostles.

We pray the Apostles' Creed and the other creeds alone and together as a Church community. Praying the creeds of the Church helps us grow as a Church family. It helps us remember who we are as a Church.

Look up and read the Apostles' Creed on page 284. Fill in the blanks with three things the Apostles' Creed professes about Jesus.

I Believe in Jesus Christ

I believe in God, the _____ almighty, creator of heaven and earth.

I believe in Jesus Christ, his only Son, our Lord.

- _____

_____

- _____

_____

- _____

_____

Our Church Makes a Difference

Living What We Believe

You have heard the saying, "Actions speak louder than words." Many people first come to know Jesus and follow him because of the deeds, or actions, of Christians.

The New Testament tells us how the first Christians lived their faith in Jesus. One writer wrote, "See how they love one another. See how they are ready even to die for one another." Many people admired the way the Christians lived their faith. They asked to be baptized and became followers of Jesus.

We not only pray the words of the creed, we also live what we say we believe. When our actions speak louder than our words, we make a difference in the world.

Name some of the ways the Christians in these pictures are living their faith. Now name one other way you can live your faith.

Our Catholic Faith

Baptism Promises

At Baptism those about to be baptized both promise to live as God's children and make a profession of faith. Every Easter we join with the whole Church and renew the promises we made at Baptism. We promise to live our faith.

221

What Difference Does Faith Make in My Life?

You belong to the community of the Catholic Church. When you live the faith of the Church, you are giving your heart to God.

Design a banner that tells who you are and what you believe as a Catholic.

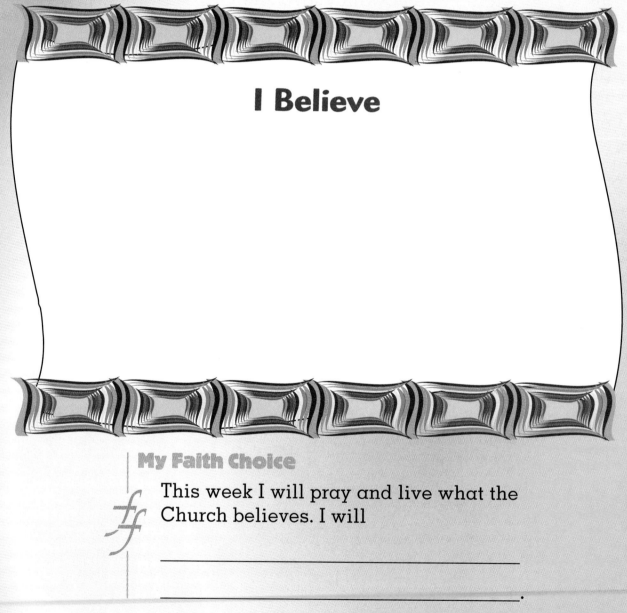

I Believe

My Faith Choice

This week I will pray and live what the Church believes. I will

_____

_____ .

You Are God

Hymns are songs of faith. The Church sings hymns to praise God and profess our faith in God. Pray this hymn together.

Group 1: You are God: we praise you;

Group 2: You are the Lord: we honor you;

Group 1: You are the eternal Father:

Group 2: All creation worships you.

Group 1: The holy Church everywhere honors you,

Group 2: Mighty Father, true and only Son, and Holy Spirit, helper and guide.

All: Come then, Lord, help your people, and bring us to everlasting life. **Amen.**

Based on the Te Deum

We Remember

Use the letters in the word PROFESS to write words about what the Church believes.

P
R
O
F
E
Holy **S**pirit
S

To Help You Remember

1. We profess what we believe about God when we pray the creeds of the Church.

2. The Apostles' Creed is a brief summary of what the Church has believed from the time of the Apostles.

3. Praying the creeds of the Church helps us grow as a Church family.

This Week . . .

In chapter 25, "We Profess Our Faith," your child learned about the creeds of the Church. The creeds of the Church summarize the faith of the Church. The Apostles' Creed is one of the main creeds of the Catholic Church. It is called the Apostles' Creed not because it was written by the Apostles but because it is a summary of the faith handed on to the early Church from apostolic times. When we profess our faith, we do not profess it simply on our own. We profess our faith in prayer with the help of the Holy Spirit.

For more on the teachings of the Catholic Church on prayer, see *Catechism of the Catholic Church* paragraph numbers 2650–2672.

Sharing God's Word

Read together the Bible passage 1 Corinthians 15:3–11. Emphasize that Paul wrote one of the earliest creeds of the Church.

Praying

In this chapter your child prayed part of the hymn "Te Deum." Read and pray together the prayer on page 223.

Making a Difference

Choose one of the following activities to do as a family or design a similar activity of your own.

- Pray the Apostles' Creed every day this week for family prayer. Praying this prayer daily will help your family grow in your identity as a Catholic family.

- Compare the Apostles' Creed and the Nicene Creed on page 284. Talk about what the two creeds have in common and how they are different from each other.

- Write a family creed. Be sure to include your beliefs about God the Father, God the Son, God the Holy Spirit, the Catholic Church, and life after death. Pray your family creed at dinnertime this week.

For more ideas on ways your family can live your faith, visit the "Faith First for Families" page at **www.FaithFirst.com**. Click on "Make a Difference." Discover ways for your family to live your faith.

The Hail Mary
A Scripture Story

26

Elizabeth greeting Mary

We Pray

"Mary, most blessed are you among women."　Luke 1:42

Holy Mary, Mother of God, pray for us.　Amen.

When have you asked someone to do a favor for you?

People turn to one another when they need help. Catholics ask Mary to pray to God for them.

What prayer asks Mary to pray for us?

Bible Background

Faith Focus

Why do we pray the Hail Mary?

Faith Words

Visitation
The Visitation is the visit of Mary, the mother of Jesus, with Elizabeth, the mother of John the Baptist.

Hail Mary
The Hail Mary is a prayer based on the Gospel stories of the Annunciation and the Visitation.

Color the stained-glass window of Mary praying.

The Annunciation

Mary and other young Jewish girls of her time first learned about their religion and customs at home. They learned God would some day send God's people the Messiah, who would be their Savior. They came to hope that one of them would be the mother of the Messiah.

Mary, like the Jewish people of her time, prayed for the coming of the Savior. The angel Gabriel came to Mary while she was praying. Gabriel greeted Mary, saying,

"Hail, you are full of grace, for God is with you." Based on Luke 1:30

The angel told Mary that God had chosen her to be the mother of the Savior. We call this the Annunciation. Mary is the mother of Jesus. Jesus is the Savior and Messiah God promised to send.

Wood carving of
Elizabeth greeting Mary

The Visitation

The angel Gabriel told Mary that her
relative Elizabeth was also going to have
a son. So Mary went to visit Elizabeth.
Here is what happened.

> When Elizabeth saw Mary, she
> greeted Mary. Elizabeth said,
> "Blessed are you among women, and
> blessed is the child you carry within
> your womb." Mary stayed with
> Elizabeth for three months and then
> returned home. Based on Luke 1:41–42, 56

The visit of the Virgin Mary to
Elizabeth is called the **Visitation.**

*Work with two partners. Prepare a role-play of
the Visitation. Act it out for your group.*

The Hail Mary

We honor Mary for her great faith. One way we show we honor Mary is by praying the **Hail Mary.** The Hail Mary has two parts. In the first part we greet and honor Mary as Gabriel and Elizabeth did.

The Church has added the second part of the prayer. In this part, we ask Mary to help us live as followers of Jesus. We pray that Mary will greet us and welcome us to heaven.

Showing Our Love for Mary

Decorate the letter H to show your love for Mary.

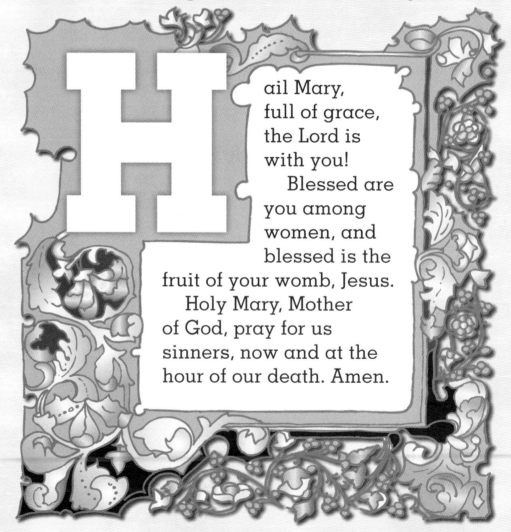

Hail Mary, full of grace, the Lord is with you! Blessed are you among women, and blessed is the fruit of your womb, Jesus. Holy Mary, Mother of God, pray for us sinners, now and at the hour of our death. Amen.

Our Church Makes a Difference

Say Yes to God

The Jewish name *Mary* means "excellence." Mary is "full of grace." She is the greatest of the saints. Mary said yes to God and became the mother of Jesus, the Son of God. That is why Mary is the Mother of God.

Throughout her whole life, Mary always gave her whole heart to God. We ask Mary to pray for us. We ask her to help us grow in our love for God. We ask her to help us say yes to God as she did.

Tell about how you join with the other people of your parish to honor Mary.

What Difference Does Faith Make in My Life?

Mary had great faith and trust in God. Mary said yes to God. It is because of your faith and trust in God that you say yes to God too.

Write a prayer asking Mary to help you say yes to God.

Saying Yes to God

_____

_____

_____

_____

_____

_____

_____

My Faith Choice

This week I will ask Mary to help me say yes to God. I will pray the Hail Mary when

_____

_____.

Mary's Prayer

Mary prayed when Elizabeth welcomed Mary to her home. Mary's prayer is called the Magnificat. Pray this part of the Magnificat together.

Leader: Let us pray the words Mary prayed.

Group 1: "My soul proclaims the greatness of God."

Group 2: "My spirit is filled with joy."

All: Hail Mary . . .

Group 3: "God has blessed me."

Group 4: "Holy is the name of God."

Based on Luke 1:46–49

All: Hail Mary . . .

We Remember

Discover the hidden message. Use the number code.

1 = A	2 = R	3 = M	4 = O	5 = L	6 = U	7 = F

"H__ i__ __a__y!
  1   5   3 2

y__ __ a__ e __ u l__
 4 6   2   7   5

o__ g__ __ ce."
 7 2 1

To Help You Remember

1. The Hail Mary remembers Mary's faith in God.

2. The Hail Mary remembers God's love for Mary.

3. The Church honors Mary by praying the Hail Mary.

This Week . . .

In chapter 26, "The Hail Mary: A Scripture Story," your child learned that Mary and other Jewish girls of her time learned about their religion and customs and prayer at home. Mary, like all her people, prayerfully waited in expectation for the coming of the Messiah God promised to send his people. When the time came for God to fulfill that promise, he sent the angel Gabriel to Mary to ask her to be the mother of his Son, Jesus. Mary, giving her whole heart to God, said yes. The Church uses the words of Gabriel and of Elizabeth in the Hail Mary.

For more on the teachings of the Catholic Church on the Hail Mary, see *Catechism of the Catholic Church* paragraph numbers 2673–2679.

Sharing God's Word

Read together the Bible story in Luke 1:26–38 about the Annunciation and the story of the Visitation in Luke 1:39–56 or read the adaptation of one of these stories on pages 226 and 227. Emphasize Mary's faith, hope, and love for God.

Praying

In this chapter your child prayed part of the Magnificat, Mary's prayer of praise of God. Read and pray together the prayer on page 231.

Making a Difference

Choose one of the following activities to do as a family or design a similar activity of your own.

- Show your respect and love for Mary as a family. Use the Hail Mary for family prayer this week.

- When you take part in Mass this week, spend some time in church after Mass. Look around for any pictures or statues of Mary. Talk about what these works of art tell us about Mary.

- Make a Hail Mary puzzle. Write the Hail Mary on a piece of paper and cut the paper into strips. Assemble the strips over and over. As you assemble the puzzle, talk about how Mary is a model of faith, hope, and love for Christian families.

For more ideas on ways your family can live your faith, visit the "Faith First for Families" page at **www.FaithFirst.com**. "Gospel Reflections" will continue to change each week over the summer. Don't forget to check it out.

A. The Best Word or Phrase

Complete the sentences. Circle the best choice under each sentence.

1. The _____ is the prayer Jesus taught his disciples.

   a. Hail Mary   b. Apostles' Creed   c. Our Father

2. The _____ is Gabriel's telling Mary that God had chosen her to be the mother of Jesus, the Son of God.

   a. Visitation   b. Resurrection   c. Annunciation

3. Jesus used the word *Abba*, which means "_____," to show his love for God the Father.

   a. Holy One   b. Almighty   c. Father

4. Praying alone is called _____ prayer.

   a. personal   b. public   c. quiet

5. Praying with others is called _____ prayer.

   a. personal   b. public   c. private

6. Prayers for ourselves are called prayers of _____.

   a. praise   b. petition   c. thanksgiving

7. When we pray the creeds of the Church, we profess our _____.

   a. faith   b. hope   c. love

8. The _____ Creed is the creed we usually profess at Mass on Sunday.

   a. Apostles'   b. Nicene   c. Catholic

B. Petitions and Intercessions

Put a ✔ in the box next to the examples of petitions.
Put an X in the box next to the examples of intercessions.

❑ "Forgive me, Lord."

❑ "Lord, help Jenny who is sick."

❑ "Give me courage, Lord."

❑ "Lord, help the leaders of the Church."

C. What I Have Learned

1. What are two new things you learned in this unit?

_____

_____

2. Look back at the list of faith words on page 200. Circle the words you now know. Tell your group the meaning of two of the words.

D. From a Scripture Story

Name the person who said these words to Mary. Put an **E** for Elizabeth. Put a **G** for the angel Gabriel.

_____ 1. "Hail, you are full of grace."

_____ 2. "God is with you."

_____ 3. "Blessed are you among women."

_____ 4. "Blessed is the child you carry within your womb."

How does the Church celebrate its faith all year long?

The Liturgical Year

We call the Church's celebration of the liturgy the liturgical year. The seasons of the liturgical year are Advent, Christmas, Lent, Easter, and Ordinary Time.

Advent
Advent begins the liturgical year. For about four weeks the Church prepares for God's coming among us. We get ready to celebrate Christmas.

Christmas
During the Christmas season, we celebrate that the Son of God came and lived among us.

prayer · fasting · almsgiving

Lent
During Lent we prepare for Easter. It is a time to prepare to welcome new members into the Church. It is a time to renew our own baptismal promises.

Triduum
Holy Thursday, Good Friday, and Easter Vigil/Easter Sunday are the most important days of the liturgical year. We call these three days the Triduum.

Easter
The Easter season lasts fifty days. We celebrate the Resurrection of Jesus from death to new life.

Ordinary Time
The other weeks of the year are called Ordinary Time. We remember Jesus' work on earth and his teachings.

Ordinary Time

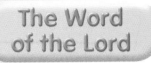
The Word of the Lord

Choose this year's Gospel reading for the Sixteenth Sunday in Ordinary Time. Read and discuss it with your family.

Year A
Matthew 13:24–43

Year B
Mark 6:30–34

Year C
Luke 10:38–42

Seasons of the Church Year

The Church has special seasons just as the calendar year does. They are times of preparation and celebration. The seasons in the Church year are Advent, Christmas, Lent, Easter, and Ordinary Time. Ordinary Time is the longest time in the Church year.

Each week of the Church year we gather at Mass to celebrate and pray. We listen to the Scripture readings to hear God's message to us. We hear about Jesus and what he taught us by his words and actions.

Each of the seasons of the Church year has a special color. During Advent and Lent the color purple or violet is used. During Christmas and Easter either white or gold is used. On some days like Palm Sunday, Good Friday, and Pentecost the color red is used. Green is the color used during Ordinary Time.

The Seasons of the Church's Year

Use the colors gold or white, purple or violet, and green that go with the different seasons of the Church's year. Color the stoles that the priest wears.

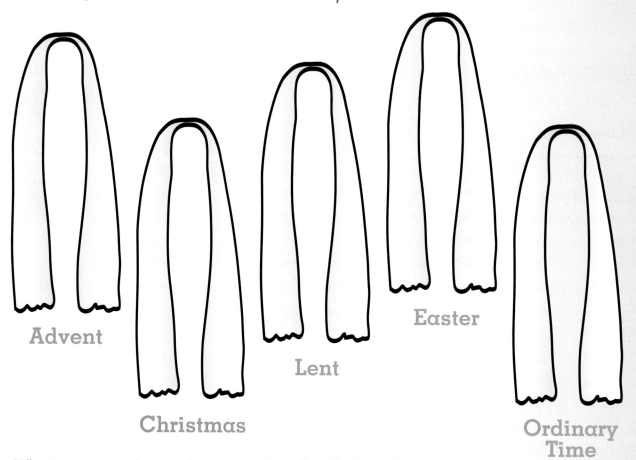

Advent

Christmas

Lent

Easter

Ordinary Time

What can you do to show your love for God during these seasons?

Season	What I Can Do
Advent	_____
Christmas	_____
Lent	_____
Easter	_____
Ordinary Time	_____

The First Week of Advent

Who are some of the people that prepared us for Jesus' coming?

The Word of the Lord

Choose this year's Gospel reading for the First Sunday of Advent. Read and discuss it with your family.

Year A
Matthew 24:37–44

Year B
Mark 13:33–37

Year C
Luke 21:25–28, 34–36

What You See

The Advent wreath is made of evergreens and four candles. Each week we light another candle as we wait for the coming of Christ at Christmastime.

A Jesse Tree

You know the names of your parents and grandparents and aunts and uncles. They are part of your family tree. A family tree helps you remember the people in your family.

During Advent we make a family tree to prepare for Christmas. It helps us remember the people who prepared the way for Jesus. We call this tree a Jesse tree. Jesse was a shepherd from Bethlehem. He was also the father of King David, an ancestor of Jesus. We hang symbols on the Jesse tree to remind us of the people who prepared the way for Jesus.

We remember Adam and Eve and Noah. We remember Abraham and Sarah and Moses and David. We remember John the Baptist, Mary, and Joseph.

Welcoming Jesus

Decorate the Christmas tree. Under each star write the name of someone who helps you prepare for the coming of Jesus at Christmas. Send each of the people you name a thank-you card.

The Second Week of Advent

Faith Focus

Who was John the Baptist?

The Word of the Lord

Choose this year's Gospel reading for the Second Sunday of Advent. Read and discuss it with your family.

Year A
Matthew 3:1–12

Year B
Mark 1:1–8

Year C
Luke 3:1–6

Prepare the Way!

Our parents and our teachers help us get ready for big celebrations. They help us prepare when someone comes to visit our home or classroom. John the Baptist helped people prepare for the coming of Jesus. When John was born, his father said,

> "And you, child, will be called prophet of the Most High,
> for you will go before the Lord to prepare his ways." Luke 1:76

John called people to prepare to receive the Messiah promised by God. Many changed their ways, and John baptized them. They waited with great hope for the Messiah. They knew he was coming soon.

Jesus, the Messiah, came. After his death and Resurrection, he returned to his Father in heaven. During Advent, we look forward to Jesus coming again in glory at the end of time.

Get Ready

There are _____ days until Christmas. How will you prepare for Christmas?

December

I can pray for

_____

by _____

_____

_____ .

I can make up with

_____

by _____

_____

_____ .

I can offer to help

_____

by _____

_____

_____ .

I can make a gift for

_____

by _____

_____

_____ .

The Third Week of Advent

Faith Focus

How does God speak to us?

The Word of the Lord

Choose this year's Gospel reading for the Third Sunday of Advent. Read and discuss it with your family.

Year A
Matthew 11:2–11

Year B
John 1:6–8, 19–28

Year C
Luke 3:10–18

The Messiah

God speaks to us in many ways. Long ago God chose good and holy people to speak in his name. We call these people prophets. Isaiah the Prophet said that God would send his people a new leader who would bring peace and justice.

Jeremiah the Prophet said that God's Promised One would be a shepherd. He would do what is right and just. Micah the Prophet said that God's Promised One would be born in Bethlehem.

The words of the prophets came true when Jesus was born. As Christmas draws near, we look forward to the peace of Christ, God's Promised One.

The Lord Is Near

Here is a prayer you and your family may use as Christmas draws near. As a family complete the prayer. Pray it together each day this week.

Leader: As we wait for the coming of Jesus, let us also prepare to welcome him.

All: **To welcome Jesus we will**

_____

_____.

Leader: You are near to us. We rejoice in you, Lord Jesus.

All: **To show our joy that Jesus is near, we will**

_____

_____.

Leader: You are near to us. We offer our prayer to you, Lord Jesus.

All: **You are near to us. We wait in hope. Amen.**

The Fourth Week of Advent

Faith Focus

How do we prepare for Jesus?

The Word of the Lord

Choose this year's Gospel reading for the Fourth Sunday of Advent. Read and discuss it with your family.

Year A
   Matthew 1:18–24

Year B
   Luke 1:26–38

Year C
   Luke 1:39–45

Mary and Elizabeth

All Is Ready

We know how to get ready to celebrate a birthday. We may decorate the house. We may bake a cake. We may wrap gifts. We may even plan a favorite meal. During the last days of Advent, we prepare our hearts to welcome Jesus. The Church invites us to read the stories of the family of Jesus.

We read about the angel Gabriel who announced the news of Jesus' birth to Mary. The angel said, "Hail, favored one! The Lord is with you" (Luke 1:28). We also read about Mary's visit with Elizabeth. Elizabeth said to Mary, "Most blessed are you among women" (Luke 1:42). We read that an angel helped Joseph to understand that Mary's child would save all people from their sins. The angel asked Joseph to take care of Mary. Joseph said yes, and he took Mary into his home.

We Are Ready

Readings from the Bible are God's word to us. When we listen to the Bible, we need to be ready to respond to God's word. Listen to these readings and tell God you are ready for Christmas.

Reader 1: Isaiah the Prophet said, "The virgin shall be with child, and bear a son, and shall name him Immanuel" (Isaiah 7:14).

All: **We are ready!**

Reader 2: Mary said, "Behold, I am the handmaid of the Lord. May it be done to me according to your word" (Luke 1:38). Mary was ready.

All: **We are ready!**

Reader 3: Elizabeth said of Mary, "Most blessed are you among women" (Luke 1:42). Elizabeth was ready.

All: **We are ready!**

Reader 4: Paul said to us, "Rejoice in the Lord always. I shall say it again: rejoice! Your kindness should be known to all. The Lord is near" (Philippians 4:4–5).

All: **We are all ready! Come, Lord Jesus!**

The First Week of Christmas

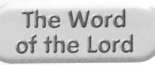

Faith Focus

How do we celebrate the arrival of Jesus?

The Word of the Lord

This is the Gospel reading for the Mass on Christmas Day. Read and discuss it with your family.

Years A, B, and C
John 1:1–18 or
John 1:1–5, 9–14

What You See

The Nativity scene (or crèche) has a new addition. It is baby Jesus! Nativity scenes usually remain on display until the feast of the Epiphany on January 6.

The Holy Family of Jesus, Mary, and Joseph

Shout for Joy!

Christmas is a time to rejoice! When Jesus was born, angels and shepherds rejoiced. The Masses for Christmas Day invite us to rejoice too.

During Christmastime we use the gifts of creation to help us rejoice. We decorate bread and cookies. We wrap packages. We put lights on our trees. We want the whole earth to rejoice and be glad. We want heaven and nature to sing.

On Christmas we rejoice. We invite the whole world to celebrate the birth of the newborn King and Savior. We remember that all creatures will happily live with one another. We read,

The wolf shall be a guest
of the lamb, . . .
The calf and the young lion shall
browse together,
with a little child to guide them.
Isaiah 11:6

A Blessing for Trees

Here is a prayer you and your family may use to bless your Christmas tree on Christmas Day.

Leader: Our help is in the name of the Lord.

All: **Who made heaven and earth.**

Reader 1: Sing to the Lord a new song. Sing to the Lord, all the earth. Bless his name; announce his salvation day after day.

All: **Sing to the Lord a new song.**

Reader 2: Let the heavens be glad and the earth rejoice; let the sea and what fills it resound; let the plains be joyful and all that is in them.

All: **Sing to the Lord a new song.**

Reader 3: Let all the trees of the forest rejoice before the Lord who comes, who comes to govern the earth.

Leader: O Lord, bless this tree. Let it shine with light. May its decorations celebrate your coming among us. We ask this in the name of Jesus your Son, born of the Virgin for us.

All: **Amen.** Based on Psalm 96:1, 2, 11–13

The Second Week of Christmas

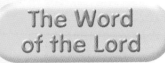

Faith Focus

Why do we call Jesus our Savior?

The Word of the Lord

This is the second reading for the Second Sunday of Christmas. Read and discuss it with your family.

Years A, B, and C
    Ephesians 1:3–6,
        15–18

What You Hear

When we celebrate Jesus' birth, we often hear the word *Alleluia*. *Alleluia* means "Praise God." We give praise to God for sending his only Son, Jesus, the Savior of the world, who saves us from sin.

Jesus Our Savior

During Christmastime we give and receive gifts. We feel happy because God's Promised One is with us. Jesus has come to be the Savior of the world. The name *Jesus* means "God saves."

The angel Gabriel told Mary that she would give birth to God's Son. His name would be Jesus because he would save his people from their sins. Later, shepherds heard angels announce that the Savior was born in Bethlehem. Some wise men, called Magi, brought gifts to the Savior.

When Mary and Joseph brought Jesus to the Temple in Jerusalem, Simeon and Anna rejoiced. Simeon blessed the child. He praised God and said,

"My eyes have seen your salvation."
                              Luke 2:30

During Christmas the Church honors Jesus as the Savior of the world. We remember that Jesus' birth is part of the great mystery of salvation.

Celebrating the Birth of Jesus

Write a poem by following these steps. Line 1: one word telling about Jesus. Line 2: the names of Jesus' mother and foster father. Line 3: three other names for Jesus. Line 4: two words about the first Christmas. Line 5: one word about your Christmas celebration.

Jesus

_____

_____   _____

_____   _____   _____

_____   _____

_____

The First Week of Lent

Faith Focus

How do we spend our time during Lent?

The Word of the Lord

Choose this year's Gospel reading for the First Sunday of Lent. Read and discuss it with your family.

Year A
Matthew 4:1–11

Year B
Mark 1:12–15

Year C
Luke 4:1–13

The Season of Lent

Think of a wonderful thing that will happen soon in your life. Will you celebrate your birthday? Will you go on a trip? Will you see a friend again? What will you do to prepare for this event?

During Lent we prepare for a wonderful happening. We get ready for Easter. We try extra hard to give time and effort to help others. We also fast, or give up something, and we try to pray more.

During Lent we also get ready to welcome new members into the Church at the Easter Vigil. We prepare ourselves to renew our baptismal promises and to become more like Jesus.

In these ways we prepare for the wonderful celebration of Easter.

On the Way to Easter

Put a ✔ next to the things in each box that you will *do* during Lent to prepare for Easter. Keep a list of all things you will do. Hang it where you will see it each day.

I will give

_____ a smile to someone who looks sad.

_____ kind words to someone who loves me.

_____ help to someone in need.

_____ thanks to someone who has helped me.

_____ other _____.

I will give up

_____ a snack during the day.

_____ a favorite TV show.

_____ arguing.

_____ a bad habit.

_____ other _____.

I will pray for

_____,

_____,

_____,

_____.

The Second Week of Lent

Faith Focus

What does it mean to be a "cheerful giver"?

The Word of the Lord

Choose this year's Gospel reading for the Second Sunday of Lent. Read and discuss it with your family.

Year A
Matthew 17:1–9

Year B
Mark 9:2–10

Year C
Luke 9:28–36

A Cheerful Giver

Sometimes we may have to give time to our younger brother or sister when we would like to play with friends. We may have to give something away that we want to keep. At these times it is not always easy to be cheerful.

During Lent we choose to give up things. Jesus asks us to be quiet and cheerful givers. He teaches us to give away money and goods without telling everyone about our good deeds. Paul the Apostle adds to this idea. He tells us, "God loves a cheerful giver" (2 Corinthians 9:7).

Jesus also asks us to fast, or give up things. He wants us to be bright and cheerful when we do this. When we fast without looking gloomy, we follow Jesus.

Jesus also asks us to pray simply and confidently to God. We pray from the deepest part of our heart. Jesus reminds us that God, our Father, knows our needs.

Be Cheerful!

Discover these Bible messages about being cheerful.
Use the code to discover the messages.

A = 1   E = 2   I = 3   O = 4   U = 5

God loves a ch __ __ rf __ l giver. (2 Corinthians 9:7)
           2 2   5

Look to God that you may be radiant with j __ y.
(Psalm 34:6)   4

A gl __ d heart lights up the face. (Proverbs 15:13)
      1

A l __ ghth __ __ rt __ d man has a continual feast.
    3   2 1   2
                          (Proverbs 15:15)

A ch __ __ rful glance brings j __ y to the heart.
      2 2   4   (Proverbs 15:30)

A j __ yf __ l heart is the health of the body.
    4   5
                          (Proverbs 17:22)

Faith Focus

Faith Focus

How do we know God is near?

The Word of the Lord

Choose this year's Gospel reading for the Third Sunday of Lent. Read and discuss it with your family.

Year A
John 4:5–42 or
John 4:5–15, 19–26,
39, 40–44

Year B
John 2:13–25

Year C
Luke 13:1–9

What You Hear

During Lent we do not sing the Alleluia. This is because we will not rejoice until we celebrate Jesus being raised from the dead on Easter.

Praying Alone and Together

We like to talk to our friends, but sometimes they are too busy. God is never too busy. God is one friend we can always talk to. We can thank and praise God and tell him our needs anytime and anywhere.

Faith tells us that God is always near. Prayer helps us to be aware that God is near. Psalm 37:7 tells us,

"Be still before the LORD;
wait for God."

During Lent we ask God to draw near us.

We are a people of prayer. On Sunday we gather to give praise and thanks to God. The Eucharist is our shared prayer to God. When we pray together, we celebrate our friendship with God.

During Lent we also pray alone. In the silence of our heart, we pray to God. When we pray alone, we celebrate our friendship with God.

The Lord Is Near

*Create the second verse to this prayer.
Sing it to the tune of "Kumbaya."*

Verse 1

    Someone's praying, Lord,
    The Lord is near.
    Someone's praying, Lord,
    The Lord is near.
    Someone's praying, Lord,
    The Lord is near.
    O Lord, you are near.

Verse 2

    Someone's _____ , Lord,
    You are here.
    Someone's _____ , Lord,
    You are here.
    Someone's _____ , Lord,
    You are here.
    O Lord, you are here.

The Fourth Week of Lent

Faith Focus

How does Jesus want us to help people?

The Word of the Lord

Choose this year's Gospel reading for the Fourth Sunday of Lent. Read and discuss it with your family.

Year A
John 9:1–41 or
John 9:1, 6–9, 13–17,
34–38

Year B
John 3:14–21

Year C
Luke 15:1–3, 11–32

A Time to Give

Sometimes we see people who need our help. Helping may not seem important to us at that time. "Someone else will help," we say.

Jesus said that when we care about people who need help, we care about him. When we feed someone who is hungry, we feed Jesus. When someone is thirsty and we offer them a drink, we offer Jesus a drink. When someone is alone or imprisoned and we visit them, we visit Jesus.

During Lent we make extra effort to help people. We remember that even the smallest things we do for those in need really do make a difference.

Saint Martin and the Beggar

Read this story. Write the ending yourself.
Clue: Read Matthew 25:35–40.

Once upon a time, Martin the soldier came upon a cold, shivering beggar on the side of the road.

Martin reined in his horse and drew his sword. He cut his wool cloak in two and gave half to the beggar.

The beggar wrapped himself in the warm cloak. He grew warm with joy and happiness.

That night Martin dreamed that Jesus stood before him on the roadway, wrapped in the part of the warm cloak Martin had given away.

Suddenly, Martin knew

_____

_____

_____ .

The Fifth Week of Lent

Faith Focus

Why is it important to forgive?

The Word of the Lord

Choose this year's Gospel reading for the Fifth Sunday of Lent. Read and discuss it with your family.

Year A
    John 11:1–45 or
    John 11:3–7, 17,
        20–27, 33–45

Year B
    John 12:20–33

Year C
    John 8:1–11

Be Reconciled

Sometimes a friend hurts our feelings. Forgiving that friend can be difficult. But Jesus shows us that God is always ready to forgive. We must always be ready to forgive also.

During Lent the Scripture readings remind us about God's forgiveness. God seeks us the way a shepherd seeks lost sheep. God rejoices like a woman who finds a lost coin. God welcomes us home the way a father welcomes his wandering child.

During Lent the Church invites us to celebrate God's forgiveness. The Church encourages us to celebrate our return to God through the sacrament of Reconciliation.

When we have been lost and alone, God rejoices at our return. God welcomes us back. We find peace with God and with one another.

Lost and Found

In a prayer of petition, we ask God for forgiveness and the help to live as children of God. Pray this prayer of petition together.

Leader: Jesus teaches us that no sin is too big for God's forgiveness.

Leader: *(Read Luke 15:8–10.)*

Reader 1: God has given us a world to care for. For wasting or misusing God's gift of creation,

All: **we ask forgiveness.**

Reader 2: God has given us friends to help and be with us. For failing to be fair and friendly in return,

All: **we ask forgiveness.**

Reader 3: God has given us grown-ups to teach and guide us. For failing to honor and obey them,

All: **we ask forgiveness.**

Reader 4: God has given us tools and toys for work and play. For failing to use them with care and thankfulness,

All: **we ask forgiveness.**

Leader: O Lord, we know you forgive us. Help us forgive others from our heart. Keep us free from sin and evil. Lead us to the joy of your kingdom, where you live and reign forever.

All: **Amen.**

Palm Sunday of the Lord's Passion

Faith Focus

What event do we remember on Palm Sunday of the Lord's Passion?

The Word of the Lord

Choose this year's Gospel reading for Palm Sunday of the Lord's Passion. Read and discuss it with your family.

Year A
    Matthew 26:14–27:66
    or Matthew 27:11–54

Year B
    Mark 14:1–15:47 or
    Mark 15:1–39

Year C
    Luke 22:14–23:56 or
    Luke 23:1–49

What You See

On this day palm branches are held high during the reading of the Passion of Our Lord. We do this to re-create and remember Jesus' entry into Jerusalem.

Hosanna!

When someone important comes to your school, you celebrate. You greet the person and do special things.

Many years ago children welcomed Jesus to Jerusalem. They did this on the day we call Palm Sunday of the Lord's Passion.

The celebration of Palm Sunday of the Lord's Passion begins Holy Week. On that day we carry palms and remember the day Jesus came into the city of Jerusalem. People welcomed him and cheered. They called out, "Hosanna!" They waved palm branches. They spread their cloaks on the road to make the path smooth and less dusty for Jesus.

Welcoming Jesus

Work with three or four partners. Practice this play. Act out the play for the whole group.

Act 1

Reader: Once Jesus welcomed children just like you. Moms and dads brought their children to Jesus to be blessed.

Apostles: Jesus is very busy. Stay away!

Jesus: No. Let the children come. The kingdom of heaven belongs to children just like these.

Act 2

Reader: Later Jesus entered the city of Jerusalem on a donkey. The children were there. They cheered and cheered for Jesus. They remembered him and offered their praises.

Children: All glory, laud and honor
To thee, Redeemer, King!
To whom the lips of children
Made sweet hosannas ring.

The Word of the Lord

Choose one of the Scripture readings for Holy Thursday. Read and discuss it with your family.

First Reading
    Exodus 12:1–8, 11–14

Second Reading
    1 Corinthians 11:23–26

Gospel
    John 13:1–15

Called to Serve

The three days just before Easter Sunday are one big celebration. They are called the Easter Triduum. The word *triduum* means "three days."

The celebration of the Easter Triduum begins on Holy Thursday with the evening Mass of the Lord's Supper. The Church remembers the first time that Jesus took bread and wine and said, "This is my body," and "This is my blood." We remember that Jesus gave us the Eucharist.

The Gospel reading tells us that Jesus washed the feet of his disciples at the Last Supper. The washing of the disciples' feet shows us that Jesus served others. All of us who share in the Body and Blood of Christ Jesus are also to serve others as Jesus did.

The Last Supper

Hands to Serve

Trace an outline of your hand over the words on this page. Think of ways to serve using your hands. Write them in the lines provided. Then say this prayer together.

Reader 1: When my hands comfort others,
All: **God is truly here.**

Reader 2: When my hands help others,
All: **God is truly here.**

Reader 3: When my hands open and close in prayer,
All: **God is truly here.**

Reader 4: When my hands hold on tight,
All: **God is truly here.**

Reader 5: _____
_____ ,
All: **God is truly here.**

Reader 6: _____
_____ ,
All: **God is truly here.**

Faith Focus

Why do we remember Good Friday?

The Word of the Lord

Choose one of the Scripture readings for Good Friday. Read and discuss it with your family.

First Reading
   Isaiah 52:13–53:12

Second Reading
   Hebrews 4:14–16,
            5:7–9

Gospel
   John 18:1–19:42

We Remember

On Good Friday we remember that Jesus died on the cross because he loved all of us. When someone is put to death on a cross, it is called a crucifixion.

Jesus was accused of being a criminal. Even though he was innocent, some people wanted him to die on the cross anyway. They shouted, "Crucify him!" The soldiers took Jesus away. They made Jesus carry his cross along the road to the place where criminals were put to death.

Jesus carrying his cross

Before Jesus died, he forgave the people who hurt him. He asked his Father to forgive them. He prayed, "Father, forgive them for they know not what they do" (based on Luke 23:34).

Whenever we see a cross or a crucifix, we thank God for loving us so much. We remember to forgive those who have hurt us.

Reminders of God's Love

Write or draw something you can do this Good Friday to thank Jesus for giving his life for you.

Why are Christians especially happy at Easter?

Choose this year's Gospel reading for Easter Sunday. Read and discuss it with your family.

Year A
John 20:1–9 or
Matthew 28:1–10 or
Luke 24:13–35

Year B
John 20:1–9 or
Mark 16:1–7 or
Luke 24:13–35

Year C
John 20:1–9 or
Luke 24:1–12 or
Luke 24:13–35

Praise the Lord!

Think of a time when something wonderful happened and you were really happy. Did you want to sing or shout or jump for joy? What happy words came to you? For Christians, *Alleluia* is a happy word.

We are Easter people. Alleluia is our song. We are people of the Resurrection.

Every Sunday we praise and thank God for the new life of the Resurrection. The responsorial psalm sung on Easter reminds us, "This is the day the Lord has made; let us be glad and rejoice in it."

During the fifty days of the Easter season, the Church sings Alleluia over and over. *Alleluia* means "Praise the Lord!" We praise God because we are new in the Lord. We walk in the light of the new day of the Resurrection.

Praise the Lord. Alleluia!

Divide into two groups. Face each other and take turns praying the verses of this psalm.

All: **Alleluia!**

Group 1: Praise the LORD from the heavens;
    give praise in the heights.

Group 2: Praise him, all you   ;
    give praise, all you hosts.

All: **Alleluia!**

Group 1: Praise him,   and   ;
    give praise, all shining   .

Group 2: You   and hail,   and   ,
    storm winds that fulfill his command;

All: **Alleluia!**

Group 1: You   and all hills,

    fruit   and all cedars;

Group 2: You   wild and tame.

    You kings of the   and all   .

All: **Praise the LORD. Alleluia!**

Based on Psalm 148:1–3, 7–11

The Second Week of Easter

Faith Focus
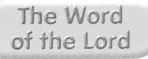

What did the first witnesses of the Resurrection tell us about Jesus?

The Word of the Lord

This is the Gospel reading for the Second Sunday of Easter. Read and discuss it with your family.

Years A, B, and C
John 20:19–31

What You See

One of the Easter symbols is the Paschal, or Easter, candle. The candle is lighted at the Easter Vigil and during the celebration of the liturgy throughout the Easter season.

Witnesses for Christ

When we witness something, we tell other people what we have seen. Many people witnessed the new life of Jesus. They told others about the Risen Lord.

Mary Magdalene saw the Risen Jesus and proclaimed the good news to the disciples: "I have seen the Lord" (John 20:18). Two other disciples knew the Risen Lord in the breaking of the bread.

The Risen Jesus appeared many times to his Apostles. He gave them peace and the gift of the Holy Spirit. Thomas the Apostle professed his faith in Jesus as his Lord and God.

These witnesses believed in Jesus as the Risen Lord. They were the first witnesses. By what you say and do, you are also a witness to the Risen Lord today.

Today's Witnesses

Mary Magdalene and Thomas the Apostle were witnesses to the Risen Lord. Draw a picture of how you can be a witness to the Risen Lord. On the line write a title for your picture.

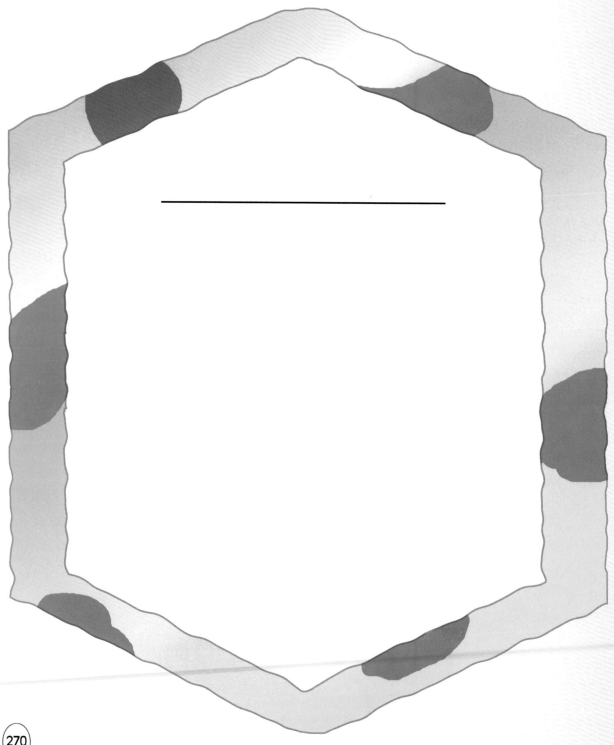

The Third Week of Easter

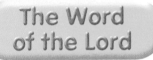
How does Jesus ask us to serve others?

The Word of the Lord

Choose this year's Gospel reading for the Third Sunday of Easter. Read and discuss it with your family.

Year A
Luke 24:13–35

Year B
Luke 24:35–48

Year C
John 21:1–19 or
John 21:1–14

Ministry

When we care for others, we minister to them. We take care of their needs and help them. Jesus asks us to do this. He asks us to serve one another.

Jesus said, "I am the good shepherd" (John 10:14). He is a leader who serves others. During the Easter season

we think about Jesus as a good shepherd. Jesus is a shepherd who gave his life for his sheep.

The first Christians ministered to those in need. They were willing to serve others as Jesus taught them to do.

During Easter we think about our faith in Jesus. We think about how living our faith in Jesus makes a difference. We think about Baptism and how we meet Jesus in the other sacraments. We think about how we can serve others as Jesus did.

Sharing in Ministry

Create a diamond-shaped poem by writing the following:

  Line 2: two words to describe "ministry"

  Line 3: three "-ing" words about how you can
    minister to others

  Line 4: four words naming skills and talents you
    have to give

  Line 5: three needs in your parish

  Line 6: two ministering people in your parish

Ministry

_____ _____

_____ _____ _____

_____ _____ _____ _____

_____ _____ _____

_____ _____

_____
(your name)

Faith Focus

What does the Eucharist call us to share?

The Word of the Lord

Choose this year's Gospel reading for the Fourth Sunday of Easter. Read and discuss it with your family.

Year A
John 10:1–10

Year B
John 10:11–18

Year C
John 10:27–30

What You See

The priest wears white vestments during the Easter season. White is a symbol of joy and life. We rejoice in Jesus' Resurrection.

Welcome to the Table

The Church welcomes new members by celebrating the three sacraments of Baptism, Confirmation, and Eucharist. The Church washes them in the waters of Baptism. The Church lays hands upon them and anoints them with oil at Confirmation. The Church invites them to share in the Body and Blood of Christ in the Eucharist.

When we celebrate the Eucharist, we participate in the Paschal Mystery. Together, we sometimes say aloud or sing,
"When we eat this bread and drink this cup, we proclaim your death, Lord Jesus, until you come in glory."

The Eucharist calls us to share our life with others. When we help others by sharing our talents, we tell others the good news of Jesus' Resurrection. We are lights in the world.

Lighting the Easter candle

Love and Serve the Lord

Read this rhyme about the celebration of the Eucharist. Then add a verse of your own. Tell how you love and serve the Lord.

The Lord's Day

Each week upon the Lord's Day,
We remember Jesus in a special way.

Many gather to sing and praise,
To hear and heed God's saving ways.

We celebrate together the great story,
How Jesus died and was raised to glory.

We share Body broken and Blood outpoured.
His gift is himself, our Savior and Lord.

The Lord we receive; the Lord we share.
We love and serve every day and everywhere.

_____

_____

The Fifth Week of Easter

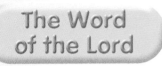

Faith Focus

How do Christians show their faith in Jesus?

The Word of the Lord

Choose this year's Gospel reading for the Fifth Sunday of Easter. Read and discuss it with your family.

Year A
   John 14:1–12

Year B
   John 15:1–8

Year C
   John 13:31–35

Faith in Action

When someone is a good leader, we follow that person. We do what our leader does. Our actions show that we are good followers. As Christians we follow Jesus.

James the Apostle says that our good words and works witness to Jesus' new life. James says that we show our faith in Jesus through our actions.

If we see someone without food or clothing, we must do something to help. James reminds us that we cannot just say, "Go in peace, keep warm, and eat well" (James 2:16). John the Apostle says the same thing. "Children, let us love not in word or speech but in deed and truth" (1 John 3:18).

Today we are called to be witnesses to the good news of Jesus' Resurrection. God calls us to put our faith into action. The Holy Spirit helps us do this.

Living Our Faith

Pretend a new family with a third grader moves into your neighborhood. Create a skit showing how you will welcome the new boy or girl. Write a title and describe two scenes for your skit.

TITLE: _____

Scene 1: _____

_____

_____

_____

_____

_____

Scene 2: _____

_____

_____

_____

_____

_____

Faith Focus

What did the followers of Jesus do to help the Church grow?

The Word of the Lord

Choose this year's Gospel reading for the the Sixth Sunday of Easter. Read and discuss it with your family.

Year A
    John 14:15–21

Year B
    John 15:9–17

Year C
    John 14:23–29

The Growing Church

When we do good, others want to do good too. When we do good, we become good news for others. That is what the followers of Jesus are. They are good news!

During the Masses of the Easter season, the first reading at Mass is from the Acts of the Apostles. We learn how the early Church grew under the guidance of the Holy Spirit.

The first followers of Jesus welcomed others. They shared food and clothing with people in need. They prayed for one another. They cared for people who were sick. People who did not believe in Jesus saw this faith in action. They wanted to do good too.

Followers of Jesus do more than talk about the good news of Jesus' Resurrection. They show that they are good news themselves! People see this. They want to follow Jesus too. The Church grows and grows.

Who's Who?

Find these passages in the Bible. Write down the name of the follower of Jesus.

I was chosen to take the place of Judas.

I am _____ .

(Acts of the Apostles 1:24–26)

I was a deacon. I gave my life for Christ.

I am _____ .

(Acts of the Apostles 7:54–60)

Once I persecuted Christians. Then I became an apostle and a missionary.

I am _____ .

(Acts of the Apostles 9:1–8)

My husband and I welcomed Paul to our home. We were tentmakers.

I am _____ .

(Acts of the Apostles 18:1–4)

Faith Focus

What is the Good News that Christians share with others?

The Word of the Lord

Choose this year's Gospel reading for the Seventh Sunday of Easter. Read and discuss it with your family.

Year A
John 17:1–11

Year B
John 17:11–19

Year C
John 17:20–26

The Risen Christ

Sharing the Good News of the Resurrection

We smile when we have good news. We share it with others. Our good news is that God has raised Jesus to new life. We share this good news by the way we live.

Before Jesus returned to his Father, he told his Apostles to share this good news with everyone. He told them to baptize and teach people. Jesus promised always to be with his followers.

After the Risen Jesus returned to his Father, the Holy Spirit came to his followers as Jesus promised. The Holy Spirit guided and helped them. They lived joyful lives. They became generous and loving. Their actions showed others that they were a joyful, generous, and loving people.

Love in Action

Jesus calls us to share the good news of his Resurrection with people. We do this both by our words and by our actions. Color in all the parts that name actions that are good news to others with one color. In the empty space write one thing you can do. Choose other colors for the rest of the boxes.

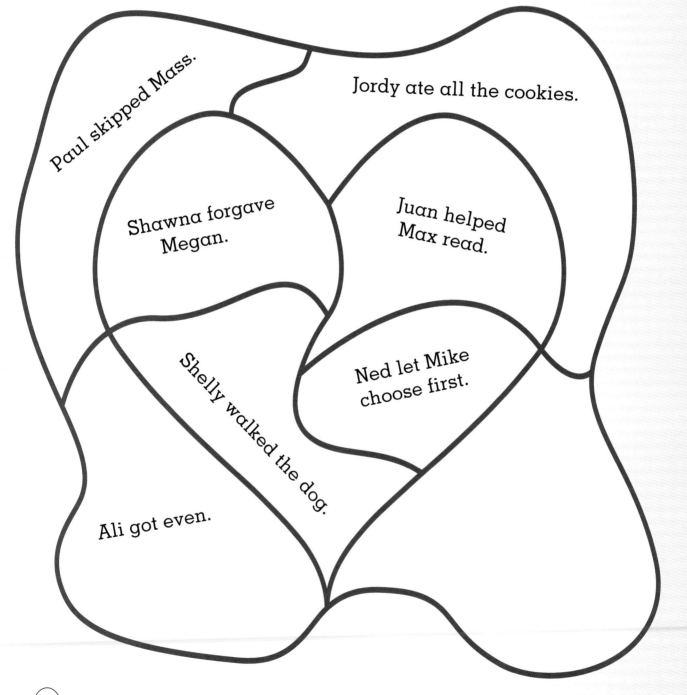

Paul skipped Mass.

Jordy ate all the cookies.

Shawna forgave Megan.

Juan helped Max read.

Shelly walked the dog.

Ned let Mike choose first.

Ali got even.

Pentecost

Faith Focus

How does the Holy Spirit help the Church?

The Word of the Lord

Choose this year's Gospel reading for Pentecost. Read and discuss it with your family.

Year A
John 20:19–23

Year B
John 15:26–27, 16:12–15

Year C
John 14:15–16, 23–26

Pentecost

When we have difficult things to do, the Holy Spirit helps us. We can depend on the Holy Spirit. We can grow in faith, hope, and love with the help of the Holy Spirit.

On the feast of Pentecost the disciples were gathered in Jerusalem. As they prayed together, they heard the sound of a great wind. Flames gently settled over their heads. Filled with the Holy Spirit, they boldly proclaimed the Risen Lord.

Peter stood in front of the people. Everyone understood his words even though everyone did not speak the same language as Peter. He told them about Jesus' life, death, and Resurrection. He wanted everyone to know that the Risen Jesus was Messiah and Lord. Many people became followers of Jesus. Those who were baptized received the Holy Spirit. They grew into the new People of God who followed the Risen Lord. The People of God is another name for the Church.

A dove, a symbol for the Holy Spirit

Come, Holy Spirit

Saint Paul tells us that we are temples of the Holy Spirit. The Holy Spirit lives within us. Pray this prayer to the Holy Spirit.

LEADER: The Holy Spirit has always been at work in the world.

GROUP 1: The spirit of the LORD shall rest
upon us:
a spirit of wisdom and
of understanding,

GROUP 2: A spirit of right judgment and courage,

GROUP 3: A spirit of knowledge and
reverence.   Based on Isaiah 11:2

ALL: **Come, Holy Spirit, fill the hearts
of your faithful.**

GROUP 1: I am David. When I was a young shepherd boy, Samuel anointed me with oil. The spirit of the Lord rushed upon me.   Based on 1 Samuel 16:12–13

GROUP 2: I am Mary. The angel told me the Holy Spirit would come upon me. I would be Jesus' mother.
                    Based on Luke 1:26–38

GROUP 3: We are the Church. Jesus told the Apostles, "I am sending the promise of my Father upon you; but stay in the city until you are clothed with power from on high."   Luke 24:49

ALL: **Come, Holy Spirit, fill the hearts
of your faithful.**

Catholic Prayers and Practices

Sign of the Cross

In the name of the Father,
and of the Son,
and of the Holy Spirit. Amen.

Glory Prayer

Glory to the Father,
    and to the Son,
    and to the Holy Spirit:
as it was in the beginning, is now,
    and will be for ever. Amen.

Lord's Prayer

Our Father, who art in heaven,
hallowed be thy name;
thy kingdom come;
thy will be done on earth
    as it is in heaven.
Give us this day our daily bread;
and forgive us our trespasses
as we forgive those who trespass
    against us;
and lead us not into temptation,
but deliver us from evil.
Amen.

Prayer to the Holy Spirit

Come, Holy Spirit, fill the hearts
    of your faithful.
And kindle in them the
    fire of your love.
Send forth your Spirit and
    they shall be created.
And you will renew the
    face of the earth.

Hail Mary

Hail Mary, full of grace,
the Lord is with you!
Blessed are you among women,
and blessed is the fruit
    of your womb, Jesus.
Holy Mary, Mother of God,
pray for us sinners,
now and at the hour of our death.
Amen.

Act of Contrition

My God,
I am sorry for my sins
    with all my heart.
In choosing to do wrong
and failing to do good,
I have sinned against you
whom I should love above all things.
I firmly intend, with your help,
to do penance,
to sin no more,
and to avoid whatever leads me to sin.
Our Savior Jesus Christ
suffered and died for us.
In his name, my God, have mercy.

Apostles' Creed

I believe in God,
   the Father almighty,
   creator of heaven and earth.

I believe in Jesus Christ,
   his only Son, our Lord.
   He was conceived by the power
      of the Holy Spirit
      and born of the Virgin Mary.
   He suffered under Pontius Pilate,
      was crucified, died, and was buried.
   He descended to the dead.
   On the third day he rose again.
   He ascended into heaven,
      and is seated at the right hand
      of the Father.
   He will come again to judge
      the living and the dead.

I believe in the Holy Spirit,
   the holy catholic Church,
   the communion of saints,
   the forgiveness of sins,
   the resurrection of the body,
   and the life everlasting. Amen.

Nicene Creed

We believe in one God,
   the Father, the Almighty,
   maker of heaven and earth,
   of all that is, seen and unseen.

We believe in one Lord, Jesus Christ,
   the only Son of God,
   eternally begotten of the Father,
   God from God, Light from Light,
   true God from true God,
   begotten, not made, one in Being
      with the Father.

Through him all things were made.
For us men and for our salvation
   he came down from heaven:

by the power of the Holy Spirit
   he was born of the Virgin Mary, and
      became man.

For our sake he was crucified under
   Pontius Pilate;
   he suffered, died, and was buried.
   On the third day he rose again
      in fulfillment of the Scriptures;
   he ascended into heaven
      and is seated at the right hand
      of the Father.
He will come again in glory to judge
   the living and the dead,
   and his kingdom will have no end.

We believe in the Holy Spirit, the Lord,
   the giver of life,
   who proceeds from the Father
      and the Son.
   With the Father and the Son he is
      worshiped and glorified.
   He has spoken through the Prophets.
We believe in one holy catholic and
   apostolic Church.
We acknowledge one baptism for
   the forgiveness of sins.
We look for the resurrection
   of the dead,
   and the life of the world to come.
   Amen.

Morning Prayer

Dear God,
as I begin this day,
keep me in your love and care.
Help me to live as your child today.
Bless me, my family, and my friends
    in all we do.
Keep us all close to you. Amen.

Grace Before Meals

Bless us, O Lord,
    and these your gifts
which we are about to receive
    from your goodness.
Through Christ our Lord.
Amen.

Grace After Meals

We give you thanks for all your gifts,
    almighty God,
living and reigning now and for ever.
Amen.

Evening Prayer

Dear God,
I thank you for today.
Keep me safe throughout the night.
Thank you for all the good I did today.
I am sorry for what I have chosen
    to do wrong.
Bless my family and friends. Amen.

A Vocation Prayer

God, I know you will call me
for special work in my life.
Help me follow Jesus each day
and be ready to answer your call.

The Beatitudes

"Blessed are the poor in spirit,
for theirs is the kingdom of heaven.
Blessed are they who mourn,
for they will be comforted.
Blessed are the meek,
for they will inherit the land.
Blessed are they who hunger
and thirst for righteousness,
for they will be satisfied.
Blessed are the merciful,
for they will be shown mercy.
Blessed are the clean of heart,
for they will see God.
Blessed are the peacemakers,
for they will be called children of God.
Blessed are they who are
persecuted for the
sake of righteousness,
for theirs is the kingdom of heaven.

"Blessed are you when they insult you
and persecute you and utter every kind of
evil against you [falsely] because of me.
Rejoice and be glad, for your reward will
be great in heaven."

Matthew 5:3–12

Corporal Works of Mercy

Feed people who are hungry.
Give drink to people who are thirsty.
Clothe people who need clothes.
Visit prisoners.
Shelter people who are homeless.
Visit people who are sick.
Bury people who have died.

Spiritual Works of Mercy

Help people who sin.
Teach people who are ignorant.
Give advice to people
who have doubts.
Comfort people who suffer.
Be patient with other people.
Forgive people who hurt you.
Pray for people who are alive and for
those who have died.

The Ten Commandments

1. I am the LORD your God: you shall not have strange gods before me.
2. You shall not take the name of the LORD your God in vain.
3. Remember to keep holy the LORD's Day.
4. Honor your father and your mother.
5. You shall not kill.
6. You shall not commit adultery.
7. You shall not steal.
8. You shall not bear false witness against your neighbor.
9. You shall not covet your neighbor's wife.
10. You shall not covet your neighbor's goods.

Based on Exodus 20:3, 7–17

Precepts of the Church

1. Participate in Mass on Sundays and holy days of obligation and rest from unnecessary work.

2. Confess sins at least once a year.

3. Receive Holy Communion at least during the Easter season.

4. Observe the prescribed days of fasting and abstinence.

5. Provide for the material needs of the Church, according to one's abilities.

The Great Commandment

"You shall love the Lord, your God, with all your heart, with all your soul, and with all your mind. . . . You shall love your neighbor as yourself."

Matthew 22:37, 39

Rosary

Catholics pray the rosary to honor Mary and remember the important events in the life of Jesus and Mary. There are twenty mysteries of the rosary. Follow the steps from 1 to 5.

5. Pray the Hail, Holy Queen prayer. Make the Sign of the Cross.

3. Think of the first mystery. Pray an Our Father, 10 Hail Marys, and the Glory Prayer.

2. Pray an Our Father, 3 Hail Marys, and the Glory Prayer.

4. Repeat step 3 for each of the next 4 mysteries.

1. Make the Sign of the Cross and pray the Apostles' Creed.

Joyful Mysteries

1. The Annunciation
2. The Visitation
3. The Nativity
4. The Presentation
5. The Finding of Jesus in the Temple

Mysteries of Light

1. The Baptism of Jesus in the Jordan River
2. The Miracle at the Wedding at Cana
3. The Proclamation of the Kingdom of God
4. The Transfiguration of Jesus
5. The Institution of the Eucharist

Sorrowful Mysteries

1. The Agony in the Garden
2. The Scourging at the Pillar
3. The Crowning with Thorns
4. The Carrying of the Cross
5. The Crucifixion

Glorious Mysteries

1. The Resurrection
2. The Ascension
3. The Coming of the Holy Spirit
4. The Assumption of Mary
5. The Coronation of Mary

Hail, Holy Queen

Hail, holy Queen, mother of mercy,
hail, our life, our sweetness,
    and our hope.
To you we cry, the children of Eve;
to you we send up our sighs,
mourning and weeping
    in this land of exile.
Turn, then, most gracious advocate,
your eyes of mercy toward us;
lead us home at last
and show us the blessed fruit
    of your womb, Jesus:
O clement, O loving, O sweet
    Virgin Mary.

Stations of the Cross

1. Jesus is condemned to death.

2. Jesus accepts his cross.

3. Jesus falls the first time.

4. Jesus meets his mother.

5. Simon helps Jesus carry the cross.

6. Veronica wipes the face of Jesus.

7. Jesus falls the second time.

8. Jesus meets the women.

9. Jesus falls the third time.

10. Jesus is stripped of his clothes.

11. Jesus is nailed to the cross.

12. Jesus dies on the cross.

13. Jesus is taken down from the cross.

14. Jesus is buried in the tomb.

Some parishes conclude the Stations by reflecting on the Resurrection of Jesus.

The Seven Sacraments

Jesus gave the Church the seven sacraments. The sacraments are the main liturgical signs of the Church. They make the Paschal Mystery of Jesus, who is always the main celebrant of each sacrament, present to us. They make us sharers in the saving work of Christ and in the life of the Holy Trinity.

Sacraments of Initiation

Baptism

Through Baptism we are joined to Christ and become members of the Body of Christ, the Church. We are reborn as adopted children of God and receive the gift of the Holy Spirit. Original sin and all personal sins are forgiven.

Confirmation

Confirmation completes Baptism. In this sacrament the gift of the Holy Spirit strengthens us to live our Baptism.

Eucharist

Sharing in the Eucharist most fully joins us to Christ and to the Church. We share in the one sacrifice of Christ. The bread and wine become the Body and Blood of Christ through the power of the Holy Spirit and the words of the priest. We receive the Body and Blood of Christ.

Sacraments of Healing

Reconciliation

Through the ministry of the priest we receive forgiveness of sins committed after our Baptism. We need to confess all mortal sins.

Anointing of the Sick

Anointing of the Sick strengthens our faith and trust in God when we are seriously ill, dying, or weak because of old age.

Sacraments at the Service of Communion

Holy Orders

Through Holy Orders a baptized man is consecrated to serve the whole Church as a bishop, priest, or deacon in the name of Christ. Bishops, who are the successors of the Apostles, receive this sacrament most fully. They are consecrated to teach the Gospel, to lead the Church in the worship of God, and to guide the Church to live holy lives. Bishops are helped by priests, their coworkers, and by deacons.

Matrimony

Matrimony unites a baptized man and a baptized woman in a lifelong bond of faithful love to always honor one another and to accept the gift of children from God. In this sacrament the married couple is consecrated to be a sign of God's love for the Church.

We Celebrate the Mass

THE INTRODUCTORY RITES

**We remember that we are the community
of the Church. We prepare to listen to the word of God
and to celebrate the Eucharist.**

The Entrance

We stand as the priest, deacon, and
other ministers enter the assembly. We
sing a gathering song. The priest and
deacon kiss the altar. The priest then
goes to the chair where he presides
over the celebration.

Greeting of the Altar
and of the People Gathered

The priest leads us in praying the Sign
of the Cross. The priest greets us, and
we say,

"And also with you."

The Act of Penitence

We admit our wrongdoings.
We bless God for his mercy.

The Gloria

We praise God for all the good
he has done for us.

The Collect

The priest leads us in praying the
Collect, or the opening prayer.
We respond, **"Amen."**

The Liturgy of the Word

God speaks to us today.
We listen and respond to God's word.

The First Reading from the Bible

We sit and listen as the reader reads from the Old Testament or from the Acts of the Apostles. The reader concludes, "The word of the Lord."
We respond,
"Thanks be to God."

The Responsorial Psalm

The song leader leads us in singing a psalm.

The Second Reading from the Bible

The reader reads from the New Testament, but not from the four Gospels. The reader concludes, "The word of the Lord." We respond,
"Thanks be to God."

Acclamation

We stand to honor Christ present with us in the Gospel. The song leader leads us in singing, **"Alleluia, Alleluia, Alleluia"** or another chant during Lent.

The Gospel

The deacon or priest proclaims, "A reading from the holy gospel according to (name of Gospel writer)."
We respond,
"Glory to you, O Lord."
He proclaims the Gospel. At the end, he says, "The gospel of the Lord."
We respond,
"Praise to you, Lord Jesus Christ."

The Homily

We sit. The priest or deacon preaches the homily. He helps the whole community understand the word of God spoken to us in the readings.

The Profession of Faith

We stand and profess our faith.
We pray the Nicene Creed together.

The Prayer of the Faithful

The priest leads us in praying for our Church and its leaders, for our country and its leaders, for ourselves and others, for the sick and those who have died. We can respond to each prayer in several ways. One way we respond is,
"Lord, hear our prayer."

The Liturgy of the Eucharist

**We join with Jesus and the Holy Spirit
to give thanks and praise to God the Father.**

The Preparation of the Gifts

We sit as the altar table is prepared and the collection is taken up. We share our blessings with the community of the Church and especially with those in need. The song leader may lead us in singing a song. The gifts of bread and wine are brought to the altar.

The priest lifts up the bread and blesses God for all our gifts. He prays, "Blessed are you, Lord, God of all creation . . ."
We respond,
　　"Blessed be God for ever."

The priest lifts up the cup of wine and prays, "Blessed are you, Lord, God of all creation . . ."
We respond,
　　"Blessed be God for ever."

The priest invites us,
　　"Pray, my brothers and
　　sisters, that our sacrifice
　　may be acceptable to God,
　　the almighty Father."

We stand and respond,
　　**"May the Lord accept the sacrifice
　　at your hands for the praise and
　　glory of his name, for our good, and
　　the good of all his Church."**

The Prayer over the Offerings

The priest leads us in praying the Prayer over the Offerings. We respond, **"Amen."**

293

Preface

The priest invites us to join in praying the Church's great prayer of praise and thanksgiving to God the Father.

Priest: "The Lord be with you."
Assembly: **"And also with you."**
Priest: "Lift up your hearts."
Assembly: **"We lift them up to the Lord."**
Priest: "Let us give thanks to the Lord our God."
Assembly: **"It is right to give him thanks and praise."**

After the priest sings or prays aloud the preface, we join in acclaiming,

"Holy, holy, holy Lord, God of power and might.
Heaven and earth are full of your glory.
Hosanna in the highest.
Blessed is he who comes in the name of the Lord.
Hosanna in the highest."

The Eucharistic Prayer

The priest leads the assembly in praying the Eucharistic Prayer. We call upon the Holy Spirit to make our gifts of bread and wine holy and that they become the Body and Blood of Jesus. We recall what happened at the Last Supper. The bread and wine become the Body and Blood of the Lord. Jesus is truly and really present under the appearances of bread and wine.

The priest sings or says aloud, "Let us proclaim the mystery of faith." We respond using this or another acclamation used by the Church,

"Christ has died, Christ is risen, Christ will come again."

The priest then prays for the Church. He prays for the living and the dead.

Doxology

The priest concludes the praying of the Eucharistic Prayer. He sings or prays aloud,

"Through him, with him, in him, in the unity of the Holy Spirit, all glory and honor is yours, almighty Father, for ever and ever."

We respond, **"Amen."**

THE COMMUNION RITE

The Lord's Prayer

We pray the Lord's Prayer together.

The Rite of Peace

The priest invites us to share a sign of peace, saying, "The peace of the Lord be with you always." We respond,
"And also with you."
We share a sign of peace.

The Fraction, or the Breaking of the Bread

The priest breaks the host, the consecrated bread. We sing or pray aloud,
"Lamb of God, you take away the sins of the world:
    have mercy on us.
Lamb of God, you take away the sins of the world:
    have mercy on us.
Lamb of God, you take away the sins of the world:
    grant us peace."

Communion

The priest raises the host and says aloud,
    "This is the Lamb of God who takes away the sins of the world.
    Happy are those who are called to his supper."
We join with him and say,
    "Lord, I am not worthy to receive you, but only say the word and I shall be healed."

The priest receives Communion. Next, the deacon and the extraordinary ministers of Holy Communion and the members of the assembly receive Communion.

The priest, deacon, or extraordinary minister of Holy Communion holds up the host. We bow and the priest, deacon, or extraordinary minister of Holy Communion says, "The body of Christ." We respond, **"Amen."** We then receive the consecrated host in our hand or on our tongue.

If we are to receive the Blood of Christ, the priest, deacon, or extraordinary minister of Holy Communion holds up the cup containing the consecrated wine. We bow and the priest, deacon, or extraordinary minister of Holy Communion says, "The blood of Christ." We respond, **"Amen."** We take the cup in our hands and drink from it.

The Prayer after Communion

We stand as the priest invites us to pray, saying, "Let us pray." He prays the Prayer after Communion. We respond, **"Amen."**

THE CONCLUDING RITES

**We are sent forth to do good works,
praising and blessing the Lord.**

Greeting

We stand. The priest greets us as
we prepare to leave. He says, "The
Lord be with you." We respond,
"And also with you."

Blessing

The priest or deacon may invite us, "Bow
your heads and pray for God's blessing."
The priest blesses us, saying,
"May almighty God bless you,
the Father, and the Son, and
the Holy Spirit."
We respond, **"Amen."**

Dismissal of the People

The priest or deacon sends us forth,
using these or similar words,
"The Mass is ended, go in peace."
We respond,
"Thanks be to God."

We sing a hymn. The priest and the
deacon kiss the altar. The priest,
deacon, and other ministers bow to the
altar and leave in procession.

The Sacrament of Reconciliation

Individual Rite

Greeting

Scripture Reading

Confession of Sins and Acceptance
  of Penance

Act of Contrition

Absolution

Closing Prayer

Communal Rite

Greeting

Scripture Reading

Homily

Examination of Conscience, a litany of
  contrition, and the Lord's Prayer

Individual Confession and Absolution

Closing Prayer

Glossary

A

Abba [page 203]
The word *Abba* means "Father" in the language Jesus spoke. Jesus used this word when he prayed to God the Father.

actual grace [page 190]
Actual grace is the grace given to us by the Holy Spirit to help us make choices to live a holy life.

Advocate [page 64]
Advocate is a name for the Holy Spirit that means "one who speaks for another person."

angels [page 30]
Angels were created by God. They have no bodies. They give honor and glory to God. Sometimes God sends angels to us as his messengers.

Annunciation [page 30]
The Annunciation is the announcement the angel Gabriel made to the Blessed Virgin Mary that God had chosen her to be the mother of Jesus, the Son of God.

Apostles [page 70]
The Apostles were the disciples of Jesus who witnessed his life, death, and Resurrection. They were chosen by Jesus to baptize and teach in his name.

Apostles' Creed [page 218]
The Apostles' Creed is a brief summary of what the Church has believed from the time of the Apostles.

Ascension [page 56]
The word *ascension* means "a going up." The Ascension is the return of the Risen Jesus to his Father in heaven forty days after the Resurrection.

B

Baptism [page 25]
Baptism is the Sacrament of Initiation in which we are joined to Christ. Through Baptism we become members of the Church and followers of Jesus, our sins are forgiven, and we receive the gift of the Holy Spirit.

Bible [page 15]
The Bible is the written word of God that the Holy Spirit helped God's people to write. The Bible is also called Sacred Scripture.

bishops [page 71]
The bishops of the Church are the successors of the Apostles.

Blessed Sacrament [page 114]
The Blessed Sacrament is a name given to the Eucharist, the real presence of the Body and Blood of Jesus under the forms of bread and wine.

Body of Christ [page 111]
The Church is the Body of Christ.

C

canticle [page 31]
A canticle is a song of praise to God.

Catholic Church [pages 16 and 72]
The Catholic Church is the Church founded by Jesus and whose leaders go back to the Apostles.

Christ [page 48]
The name *Christ* means "the Anointed One" and "Messiah."

Christians [page 9]
People who are baptized and believe in Jesus Christ.

Church [page 70]
The Church is the People of God. It is the Body of Christ and the temple of the Holy Spirit.

Communion of Saints [page 86]
The Communion of Saints is the community of the faithful followers of Jesus, both those living on earth and those who have died.

Confirmation [page 99]
Confirmation is the Sacrament of Initiation in which baptized people receive and celebrate the strengthening of the gift of the Holy Spirit within them.

contrition [page 135]
Contrition is the sorrow we feel when we have done something wrong.

conversion [page 80]
The experience of changing one's heart and turning back to God is called conversion.

297

Covenant [page 158]

The Covenant is the solemn agreement of friendship made between God and his people.

covet [page 174]

To covet means to wrongfully want something that belongs to someone else.

creation [page 22]

Creation is all that God has made out of love and without any help.

creeds [page 218]

Creeds are statements of what a person or a group believes.

crucified [page 54]

To be crucified means to be put to death on a cross.

Crucifixion [page 54]

The Crucifixion is the death of Jesus on the cross.

D-E

diocese [page 73]

A diocese is a local church, or church in a particular area. A diocese has many parish churches and is led by a bishop.

disciple [page 48]

A disciple is a person who learns from and follows the teachings of another person. The people who followed Jesus were called his disciples.

divine Providence [page 22]

Divine Providence is God's caring love for all his creation.

Easter [page 99]

Easter is the time of the year Christians celebrate and remember the Resurrection of Jesus.

Easter Triduum [page 99]

The Easter Triduum (or "three days") is the center of the liturgical year. It begins on Holy Thursday evening and ends on Easter Sunday evening.

Eucharist [page 114]

The Eucharist is the sacrament in which the Church gives thanks to God and shares in the Body and Blood of Christ.

eternal [page 53]

The word *eternal* means "forever."

Evangelists [page 15]

The writers of the four Gospels are called the Evangelists. Their names are Saint Matthew, Saint Mark, Saint Luke, and Saint John.

F-G

faith [page 14]

Faith is a gift from God. It helps us believe in God and all that he has revealed.

feasts [page 23]

Feasts are special days of the Church's year on which we honor the saints.

forgive [page 53]

To forgive is to pardon someone for the wrong they have done.

fruits of the Holy Spirit [page 65]

The fruits of the Holy Spirit are twelve signs that the Holy Spirit is working in the Church. They are love, joy, peace, patience, kindness, goodness, generosity, gentleness, faithfulness, modesty, self-control, and chastity.

Good Friday [page 99]

Good Friday is the Friday before Easter Sunday. It is the day when we remember Jesus was crucified and died.

Gospels [page 15]

The Gospels are the first four books of the New Testament.

grace [page 190]

God's grace is the gift of God making us sharers in the life of the Holy Trinity. It is also the help God gives us to live a holy life.

Great Commandment [page 158]

The Great Commandment is the commandment of love that all of God's laws depend on.

H-I

Hail Mary [page 226]

The Hail Mary is a prayer based on the Gospel stories of the Annunciation and the Visitation.

heaven [page 190]

Heaven is eternal life, or living forever, in happiness with God after we die.

hell [page 192]

Hell is life separated from God forever after death.

Holy Family [page 47]

The Holy Family is the family of Jesus, Mary, and Joseph.

Holy Orders [page 146]

Holy Orders is the sacrament in which a baptized man is ordained a bishop, priest, or deacon to serve the whole Church his whole life long.

Holy Spirit [page 62]

The Holy Spirit is the third Person of the Holy Trinity.

Holy Trinity [page 14]

The Holy Trinity is the mystery of one God in three divine Persons—God the Father, God the Son, and God the Holy Spirit.

honor [page 17]

Honor means "to show respect and love for someone."

Incarnation [page 30]

The Incarnation is the Son of God becoming a man and still being God.

intercession [page 210]

The word *intercession* means "to make a request for someone else."

Jerusalem [page 46]

Jerusalem is the holiest city of the Jewish people.

Jesus [page 46]

The name *Jesus* means "God saves." Jesus is the Son of God and the Savior who God promised to send his people.

Joseph [page 47]

Joseph is the foster father of Jesus and the husband of Mary.

kingdom of God [page 48]

The time when people will live in peace and justice with God, one another, and all of God's creation is known as the kingdom of God.

Last Supper [page 54]

The Last Supper is the meal that Jesus and his disciples ate together on the night before he died.

Law of Moses [page 78]

The Law of Moses is the Ten Commandments plus other important laws that guide the Jewish people in living the Covenant.

liturgical year [page 98]

The liturgical year is the cycle of seasons and feasts that make up the Church's year of worship.

liturgy [page 98]

The liturgy is the Church's work of worshiping God.

Liturgy of the Eucharist [page 115]

The Liturgy of the Eucharist is the second part of the Mass.

Liturgy of the Word [page 115]

The Liturgy of the Word is the first part of the Mass.

Lord's Prayer [page 203]

The Lord's Prayer is another name for the Our Father. It is the prayer that Jesus gave us.

Magnificat [page 31]

The Magnificat is Mary's canticle of praise to God.

Mary [page 30]

The Virgin Mary is the mother of Jesus, the Son of God who became like us.

Mass [page 9]

Mass is the celebration of listening to God's word and giving thanks and praise to God for the gift of Jesus.

Matrimony [page 146]

Matrimony is the sacrament in which a baptized man and a baptized woman make lifelong promises to serve the Church as a married couple.

Messiah [page 46]

The word *messiah* means "anointed one." Jesus is the Messiah, the Anointed One of God, the Savior God promised to send.

miracle [page 138]

A miracle is a sign of God's presence and power at work in the world.

missionaries [page 81]
Christian missionaries often travel to countries different from their own to teach about Jesus.

mystery of God [page 14]
We say that God is a mystery because we can never fully know God. God has to reveal, or tell us, about himself.

Nativity [page 32]
The Nativity is the story of the birth of Jesus.

New Testament [page 15]
The New Testament is the second main part of the Bible. It tells us about Jesus, his teachings, and the early Church.

O-P

obey [page 174]
To obey means to choose to follow the guidance of someone who is helping us live according to God's laws.

Old Testament [page 15]
The Old Testament is the first main part of the Bible. It tells the story of God's people who lived before Jesus was born.

Ordinary Time [page 100]
Ordinary Time includes the weeks of the liturgical year that are not part of the seasons of Advent, Christmas, Lent, or Easter.

Our Father [page 203]
Another name for the Lord's Prayer is the Our Father.

parables [page 122]
Parables are stories that Jesus told to help people understand and live what he was teaching.

Paschal Mystery [page 54]
The Paschal Mystery is the Passion, death, Resurrection, and Ascension of Jesus Christ.

Passover [page 47]
Passover is the feast that the Jewish people celebrate each year to celebrate God's freeing his people from slavery in Egypt.

patron saints [page 191]
Saints who have been chosen to pray in a special way for people, countries, parishes, and for other reasons are called patron saints.

penance [page 106]
A penance is a prayer or good deed that the priest in the sacrament of Reconciliation asks us to do.

Pentecost [page 62]
Pentecost is the day on which the Holy Spirit came to the disciples of Jesus in Jerusalem fifty days after the Resurrection.

People of God [page 70]
The Church is the People of God.

personal prayer [page 202]
Personal prayer is spending time alone with God.

petition [page 210]
The word petition means "to make a solemn request."

pray [page 201]
To pray is to talk and listen to God.

prayers of blessing [page 25]
Prayers of blessing are prayers in which we honor God as the Creator of everything good and the source of all our blessings.

prayers of intercession [page 210]
Prayers of intercession are prayers in which we ask God to help others.

prayers of petition [page 210]
Prayers of petition are prayers in which we ask God to help us.

prayers of praise [page 213]
Prayers of praise are prayers in which we show our love and respect for God.

prayers of thanksgiving [page 212]
Prayers of thanksgiving are prayers in which we thank God for every blessing.

psalms [page 182]
The Psalms are prayer songs found in the Bible in the Book of Psalms in the Old Testament.

public prayer [page 202]
Public prayer is praying with other people.

purgatory [page 87]
Purgatory is growing in love for God after we die so we can live forever in heaven.

Reconciliation [page 131]
Reconciliation is the sacrament that brings us God's forgiveness and mercy. This sacrament is also called the sacrament of Penance.

respect [page 10]
Respect means "to look up to," "to honor," or "to admire."

Resurrection [page 55]
The Resurrection is God the Father's raising Jesus from the dead to new life by the power of the Holy Spirit.

sacraments [page 106]
The sacraments are the seven special signs that make Jesus present to us and make us sharers in the life of the Holy Trinity.

Sacraments at the Service of Communion [page 147]
The Sacraments at the Service of Communion are Matrimony and Holy Orders.

Sacraments of Healing [page 130]
Reconciliation and Anointing of the Sick are the two Sacraments of Healing.

Sacraments of Initiation [page 106]
Baptism, Confirmation, and Eucharist are the Sacraments of Initiation.

Sacred Scripture [page 15]
The words *Sacred Scripture* mean "holy writings." Sacred Scripture is also called the Bible.

sacrifice [page 54]
To sacrifice is to give something that we value to God out of love.

saints [page 86]
The saints are people whose love for God is stronger than their love for anyone or anything else.

sanctifying grace [page 190]
Sanctifying grace is the grace we receive at Baptism. It makes us holy. It is the gift of God's sharing his life with us.

sin [page 130]
Sin is freely choosing to do or say something that we know is against God's Law.

soul [page 23]
Our soul is that part of us that lives forever. It gives us the power to know, love, and serve God.

stewards [page 182]
Stewards are people who have the responsibility to care for things and to use them well.

tabernacle [page 116]
The tabernacle is the special place in which the Blessed Sacrament is kept.

Ten Commandments [page 166]
The Ten Commandments are the laws God gave to Moses on Mount Sinai. They guide us to love God and love others as we love ourselves.

Temple in Jerusalem [page 47]
The Temple in Jerusalem is the holy place where the Jewish people worshiped God.

temple of the Holy Spirit [page 70]
The Church is the temple of the Holy Spirit.

trust [page 38]
To trust someone is to know that what the person tells us is true and that the person will always do what is good for us.

Visitation [page 226]
The Visitation is the visit of Mary, the mother of Jesus, with Elizabeth, the mother of John the Baptist.

vocation [page 146]
Our call from God to share in Jesus' life and work is called our vocation. We live this call in many ways.

works of mercy [page 73]
The works of mercy guide the Church in living as God's holy people. They guide us in caring for the needs of both the body and soul.

worship [page 98]
Worship is the adoration and honor we give to God.

Index

A-B

Abba, 203
Abraham, 166
actual grace, 190
Advent, 98,101, 236, 239–246
Angelus, 36
Anna and Simeon, 46, 249
Annunciation, 30, 33, 101
Anointing of the Sick, 106, 132, 135
Apostles, 16, 70, 71, 78, 107, 131
Apostles' Creed, 87, 218, 220, 284
Ascension, 56

Baptism, 58, 71, 74, 88, 99, 106–107, 111, 146, 149
Beatitudes, 286
Bible, 15, 37, 47, 50, 157
bishops, 71, 73, 108, 147
Blessed Sacrament, 114, 116, 119–120
Body and Blood of Christ, 88, 114–115, 119

C

Cana, 137–139, 143–144
canticle, 31
cathedrals, 169
Catholic Church, 16, 69, 71, 73, 76, 205, 222
Catholic Relief Services, 149
children of God, 86
Christmas, 98, 101, 236, 247–250
Church, 69–76, 85–92
    becoming member of, 71, 74, 88, 107
    as Body of Christ, 70, 75, 84, 88, 92
    as Communion of Saints, 85–92
    as Easter people, 267–268
    early days of, 16, 169, 221, 277
    family as domestic, 177
    as People of God, 69–76
    as people of prayer, 205, 209–216, 256
    as temple of Holy Spirit, 70, 72, 75
    work of, 69–75, 98
collection at Mass, 141
Communion of Saints, 85–92
Confirmation, 99, 106, 108, 111
contrition, 135
conversion, 80
Corporal Works of Mercy, 286
Covenant, 78, 158–159, 168
covet, 174, 176
creation, 21–27, 182–187
creeds, of Church, 19, 217–223
crucifix,109, 205, 266
Crucifixion, 54, 265

D-E

David, King, 239
deacons, 71, 147
diocese, 73
disciples of Jesus, 48
divine Providence, 22, 24
domestic church, 177

Easter, 98–99, 101, 236, 267–280
Easter candle, 57, 193, 269
Easter Triduum, 99, 103–104, 236, 263–267
Easter Vigil, 99, 252, 269
Elect, the, 99
Esther, Queen, 39
eternal life, 53–56, 87, 191–195
Eucharist, 99, 106, 113–120, 263–264, 293–295
Eucharistic Prayer, 294
Evangelists, 15

F-G-H-I

faith, 13–20, 30–35, 37–40, 43, 219, 221, 246, 277–278
family, Christian, 170, 177
fasting during Lent, 251, 254
feast days of saints, 33, 86, 89, 90
feasts of the Lord, 101
forgiveness, 53, 83, 107, 124–127, 129–131, 133–135, 210, 259–260
fruits of the Holy Spirit, 65
Funeral Mass, 193

Gabriel, angel, 29–30, 46, 226–227, 249
Galilee, 55, 139
God, Father and Creator, 21–28, 182–187. See also Holy Spirit, Holy Trinity, Jesus Christ.
Good Friday, 99, 101, 265–266
Gospel, 15, 32, 100
grace, 190, 194, 195
Great Commandment, 158–163, 287
greed, 176

Hail Mary, 29, 225–231, 283
Hannah, 38
heaven, 54–56, 86–87, 89, 92, 189–195
hell, 192
Holy Childhood Association, 49
Holy Communion, 88, 115–116
holy days of obligation, 117
Holy Family, 46–47
Holy Orders, 106, 146–147
Holy Spirit, 61–68
    Church as temple of, 70, 72
    coming upon disciples, 63, 281
    in life of Christians, 70, 72, 107–108, 110, 134, 150, 162, 186, 190, 194, 206, 214, 218–219, 276
    prayer to, 282, 283
    symbols for 72

Holy Thursday, 99, 263–264
Holy Trinity, 14, 19, 62, 168
Holy Week, 261–266
humility, 124–125, 127–128

image of God, people as, 23, 177
Incarnation, 30, 32, 35
incense, 193
Isaac, 38
Isaiah the Prophet, 243, 246, 247
Israelites, 166

J

jealousy, 176
Jeremiah the Prophet, 243
Jerusalem, 47, 54, 62, 79, 261, 281
Jesse Tree, 239
Jesus, meaning of name, 46, 249
Jesus Christ, 45–52, 53–60, 137–144
    announcement of birth of, 30, 245
    Ascension of, 56, 59, 60, 62
    birth of, 32, 247–248
    death of, 53–55, 57, 59, 60
    entry of, into Jerusalem, 261–262
    finding of, in Temple, 47
    as Good Shepherd, 271
    as Messiah, 46, 48, 51, 241–244
    miracles of, 137–144
    at prayer, 202–204
    preparing way for coming of, 239–246
    presentation of, in Temple, 46, 249
    promise of, to send Holy Spirit, 61–62, 64
    Resurrection of, 53–55, 57, 59, 60, 98
    as Savior, 31–32, 46, 53–55, 98, 101, 249–250
    as Son of God, 19, 30, 32, 35, 45–46, 48, 51, 101, 219
    as Teacher, 48, 157–164, 197–208
John Paul II, Pope, 133
Joseph of Arimathea, 55

K-L-M

kingdom of God, 48–51

Last Supper, 54, 62, 114–115, 119, 146, 191, 263
Law of Moses, 78.
Lent, 57, 98, 101, 236, 251–260
life, human, 22–23, 175
liturgical year, 97–104, 236, 235–282
liturgy, 98
Liturgy of the Eucharist, 293–295
Liturgy of the Word, 116, 292
Lord's Day, 167, 171
Lord's Prayer, 203, 207, 283

Credits